MAGNA

MASTER YOUR EMOTIONS

Title: Magna, Master Your Emotions
All Rights Reserved 2024
Dr. Elizabeth R. Vlijt
Zafiro Publishing House

ISBN: 9789083252735

Writing Coach:
Drs. Luisette Kraal
Saved To Serve International Ministry (SSIM)

CONTENTS

PART ONE:
EMOTIONS DECEIVE US

PART TWO:
DISTURBING EMOTIONS.

PART THREE:
THE WOMAN, HER DESIRES & HER GOALS

ACKNOWLEDGMENTS

Before thanking anyone, I want to acknowledge that if I am able to do anything good, it is not because of myself, but because God in His mercy has set His eyes on me, has bestowed His grace, His love, and a seed of life that can be transmitted through this book.

Thank you, Jesus, for meeting me that afternoon to give me life and save me.

I want to thank my husband, the man I love. He has always encouraged me to write even when I've gone through difficult moments as a writer. He has been more than a support for me; and I know that if it weren't for him, I wouldn't have gotten as far as I have.

Thank you, my love, for helping me understand that it is possible to believe in dreams.

I want to thank all those who, in one way or another, have contributed to the completion of this project. I can't mention names because this page wouldn't be enough to list them all, but my friends know who they are, as well as my collaborators.

Thank you, friends, for everything.

And finally, I want to thank Neftalí and Abigail, my children. They are the reason I always feel like a blessed woman with the wonderful family that God has given me.

FOREWORD

Before I even started reading this book, it had already been a blessing in my life. You might wonder why. The reason is that not long before, I had attended some special women's meetings where Elizabeth shared parts of the book during those gatherings.

During those meetings, my life was tremendously blessed, and it continued to be so as I read the book.

What impacted me the most about the book was how the characters from the Bible come to life. In the book, they are presented in a real and relatable way.

Many times, we read the Bible and see different characters in it, but we forget that each of these characters had a life not far from resembling our own today.

In "Magna, Direct the Course of Your Emotions," we see that each woman is presented from a human point of view: like the lives of Mary Magdalene, Liz, Iris, Joaida, and other characters in the book.

These are experiences of women that fit perfectly with our current reality.

A special case for me was that of Sofía and Josefa, as it touched my soul and made me realize how often we are indifferent to the pain of others.

I thought that maybe we wouldn't identify with the main character of this book, but perhaps we would identify with some of the secondary characters.

Each part of the book is very comprehensive and will help us examine ourselves, be more honest with our inner selves, and understand that there is someone who knows us exactly as we are and is willing to heal our hearts, no matter how deep the wound may be.

In the final part of the book, Elizabeth shares a revelation from God about the condition of women, but also the interpretation and how you can achieve victory in your life.

For me, this book was and still is a blessing in my life, and I hope it will be the same for yours.

Pastora Pilar Job

PREFACE

As women, we have a gift in life: we feel and are beautifully sentimental and emotional beings.

This gift must be mastered and guided to a safe conclusion. If we allow ourselves to be led by our emotions or our hormones, we will not reach the desired destination.

The purpose of writing all these fascinating stories is for you to understand some of the emotions that make us suffer and, at times, cause us to lose our way in life.

By reading this book, you will be able to move forward despite these feelings. You will understand that you are not the only woman who suffers; we all suffer. The difference lies in what you do with your pain.

The key is not to give up or let your emotions drive your life. If you truly take control of what you feel and do not let yourself be guided by chance, you will achieve the success you seek.

This book will be divided into three parts.

In the first part, we will analyze emotions by focusing on a central character. This character is Mary Magdalene. We will see how emotions deceive and confuse us, how they make us see things in the wrong way.

In the second part, we will explore feelings that trouble the soul. We will look at how different women who suffered for various reasons found answers to their lives, although not all had a happy ending, as that depends on the decisions they made in life.

In the third part, we will analyze a dream that God gave me and its interpretation. We will also look at some points to learn how to handle failure.

PART ONE:

EMOTIONS DECEIVE US

In this first part, we will analyze how the feelings we experience are often deceptively misleading, causing us to feel incorrectly.

This section will be dedicated to a single character: Mary Magdalene.

Yes, emotions deceive us, blind us, and prevent us from seeing the situation as God wants us to see it.

CHAPTER 1

Even though we may be strong in the face of adverse circumstances, we cannot control what happens in our lives. However, we can move forward despite our pain and the uncertainty of what we are going through in our difficult moments.

The pain, the tears, and the loss.

What had happened was the best thing for Mary Magdalene, but her pain did not allow her to understand that.

In her human mind, she could only remember the last scenes of the cross.

"His voice wasn't the same," she thought. She had in her mind the bloodied face of her teacher, the nails, the crowd that accused him, and that cry of thirst that Jesus had made while hanging on the cross.

That cry of thirst from her teacher echoed in her troubled mind.

She felt guilty for not being able to do anything for him.

In her head, she had the image of a defeated Christ, a teacher conquered and condemned by his own people.

It was an event she never expected from her teacher, whom she loved so much.

She had seen how her Lord bled from the lashes.

She had suffered with him.

Magdalene felt shattered, troubled, and even though her body was tired since she hadn't slept in the last three days, she didn't want to go home as the others had already done. She stood in front of the tomb searching for an answer she couldn't find but believed she would.

She couldn't understand why he had allowed himself to be killed if he had power over death.

"He had the power," she said through sobs to Salome, who was trying to convince her to go home. "I'll stay; go on, I

want to be alone," were Magdalene's words to her friend
Salome.

Her body was warm, her clothes still stained with blood
from the day of the crucifixion. Her eyes were downcast,
her hair disheveled and falling over her face, and her gaze
was lost in front of the tomb, searching for an answer.

Magdalene wanted to be alone with her pain. She didn't
want to see anyone or be with the group. She just wanted
to cry and try to understand what had happened.

"Why, why?" she said. "What am I going to do now? Where
will I go? Why did he have to die?"

CHAPTER 2

A soul that is troubled and weary tends to forget things.

Don't focus on the magnitude of your pain, but on what you can do to move forward. Try to remember the good things that have happened to you and what you have overcome to get where you are. Only by moving forward can you break the circle of your pain.

The circle of pain.

She had so many unanswered questions, and her pain was so great that she had forgotten that Jesus was God, that He had the power to rise from the tomb, as He Himself had said on several occasions. She couldn't remember this, not even when the angels reminded her.

Her pain overshadowed the answers that God had sent to comfort her.

God had moved the stone with the intention that both she and the other women would see that He was not there. God had created visible evidence to show them that He was not where they were looking for Him. God sent a pair of angels to give them the message that Jesus was not among the dead, that He was alive.

But even this method from God did not break the circle of her pain. Even when the angels spoke to them and told them that He was no longer among the dead.
Her pain made her forget that her Lord, whom she loved, was God, and therefore death could not hold Him.

Her emotions made her think of her teacher as a lifeless corpse, incapable of defending Himself from vile thieves. That whirlwind of emotions made her think that Jesus needed the few strengths of a weak woman to carry Him back to the tomb.

She had good intentions, but she was mistaken because she believed she could carry God.
Of course, she thought of Him as a corpse.
Pain robs us of the true perspective of what is really happening around us. We confuse what we feel with what we can actually do as humans.

Pain prevents us from seeing things as God wants us to see them, even when God does everything to provide evidence that what we think is not our true reality.

Pain is a way of expressing our emotions, but it often deceives us, manipulates us, and makes us think wrongly, just as it did with Magdalene.

Pain is a poor counselor. Many people who end up committing suicide do so because of pain.

Our adversary knows this; that's why he tries to produce pain in people's lives, so that they lose hope and the desire to live.

He wants you to think that no one cares about you, that everything is completely lost. He wants you to think that you cannot go on. He works to change the lens through which you view your life, making you see life through the lens of hopelessness. This lens is very dangerous; it's called discouragement, and it wants you to focus your life on the negative, on things that seem dark and gray when in reality they are colorful because our Lord lives and is at the right hand of God—did you know that?

CHAPTER 3

Pain makes us think that God is unstable.

Pain makes us see God incorrectly. It makes us measure Him by the circumstances of life. It makes us believe that there's nothing more that can be done and, worst of all, that we have to carry God... Incredible, but it's true. There are times when we think we can do things better than God and, even worse, that we should help Him so things don't fall apart.

When I read this passage myself, I was surprised—weren't you?

I wonder if I should continue with this topic; it's so harsh, but I believe it's the truth about our situation. Sometimes,

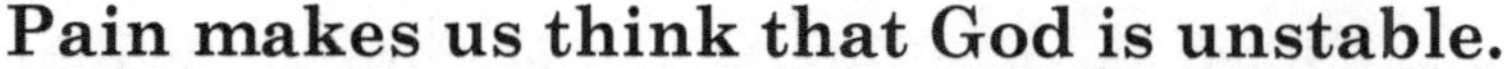

when read or said in this way, it really sounds a bit hard to accept, but I invite you to meditate for a moment. How many times have you made God so small that you think He needs your help? How many times have you wanted, like Magdalene, to carry Him to the tomb? Are you aware that your God is alive?

If so, say hallelujah. Come on, say hallelujah out loud. Hallelujah.

We think that God can't do anything on His own and that, out of love for Him, we must carry Him from where He's been placed (according to us) and take Him to where the dead rest. A human way of thinking, don't you think?

We think that God is so weak that He can be moved against His will and according to the will or desire of humans. This is where we go wrong when we think, "Maybe God wants me to do this."

We think that by following the path our pain wants to lead us on, and accepting everything our feelings suggest, we are doing what God wants. But that's not the case. It's what our carnal minds, fed by the enemy, want us to do.

The enemy doesn't want us to understand God's purpose in allowing things in our lives. That's why he tries to trap us in our own pain, making us think that we are the most suffering people in this world, that our lives are utterly miserable and hopeless.

In the past, Magdalene had been a puppet of the devil. He had used her, harmed her, and possessed her. But Jesus had freed her from the power of the evil one. This is what the devil wanted Magdalene to forget. Now he had a plan to reclaim her, which is why he was making her think wrongly and preventing her from perceiving her teacher's resurrection.

Magdalene was filled with anger and pain. She cried out of the helplessness she felt at not being able to do anything. She cried for the pain of her teacher, for all that her teacher had suffered, and for the fact that now, according to her, He wasn't being left in peace, even in death.

She wasn't afraid of someone from the guard seeing her there; in fact, I believe that's what she wanted—to ask them about her teacher. She even asked Jesus Himself, almost certain of what she was asking.

Magdalene wasn't the only one who went to the tomb. She wasn't the only one who mourned her teacher. She wasn't the only one who heard the angels, and she wasn't the only one who cried. But it seems to me that of all the women, Jesus had given the most to her. After all, Jesus had once said, "He who is forgiven much, loves much," and it seems to me that Magdalene was one of those.

She mourned the loss of her friend, her teacher, her Lord, who had freed her. The only one who understood her, who knew how to fill her emptiness, who knew what had harmed her, the one who had given her victory over her enemy.

Now, how was she supposed to move forward without Him? What would she say to all those to whom she had spoken about how magnificent her teacher was?

She hadn't understood the purpose of Jesus's death. She didn't understand why she had to go through this. Do you understand your pain, your situation, and circumstances?

Magdalene was crying for herself because, in Jesus, she had found a reason to live.

That death was a disgrace to her; maybe she would have preferred that Jesus show His power to everyone, after all, He was the only Son of God, and she knew that.
She knew He had power over death, she knew He was almighty, she knew that nothing was impossible for Him. The question was;
Why then did He allow Himself to be killed? Why didn't He do anything to stay with her?

Have you ever asked yourself the same thing?
Of course, I have, countless times, and on occasions, I've even cried like Magdalene, not understanding what God is doing, and also out of shame for what my so-called "friends" would say.
But God has used this to teach me that even when I think everything is lost, He is still doing something, even if I can't see or feel it.

Remember, spiritual things don't have to be seen or felt; they just have to be believed.

PART TWO:

DISTURBING EMOTIONS.

Cry: "To shed tears as a result of a very intense and vivid emotion."

In this second part, we will study the manifestations of these kinds of emotions that make us cry, but we will examine them in people like you and me. Afterward, we will have a section called "Reflection," where I will explain whom we have talked about, analyze the story you have just read, and then offer some advice to help with such situations.

The "Reflection" will be located at the end of each chapter in this section.
The purpose of "Reflection" is to shed light on the story you have just read.

Women cry because there are feelings that disturb them, and many times they don't know how to, or can't, confront these feelings.

This second part will be dedicated to common stories of women who went through situations similar to what you and I face today.

Some of the feelings we will study include:

Frustration, discouragement, rejection, insecurity, fear, exhaustion, heartbreak, and others, but we will look at them through real stories.

I have tried to understand the tears of some women, including my own.

To be honest, I haven't seen many women cry; but the few I have seen left me with a bitter memory.

One of the women I saw cry was Ager. I saw her cry because she didn't want to die and leave her daughters as orphans.

She never told me her story; but after she died, I found out some things that explained why I had seen her cry, or suffer, to put it more understandably.

Ager's story, as I will call her, is a bit sad.

Ager is our first character in this section. In her, we will study frustration and heartbreak.

CHAPTER 4

There are circumstances in life that we never chose. We were born into a home we didn't choose, a culture we didn't choose, parents we didn't choose, and the truth is that many things that happen to us were not our choice when we were still defenseless children. All of this is true, but it is also true that we can grow up, rise above, and stop being victims in our minds. We can try to change the seeds of pain, rejection, and abuse that were planted in us so that they have less effect on our lives. Get up and stop being a victim; seek help, heal, and learn to live.

Broken dreams and withered hopes.

Ager was a young girl with a desire to live just like any

other young person of that time. I'm talking about the early 1960s. She was about 13 years old, and she didn't know much about life or relationships with men.

Even at 13, she groomed herself like a child, thought like a child, and played like a child. She still played with dolls and ran around with her neighborhood friends, unaware of what life had in store for her.

That week was like any other, except for the visit to her parents by an older man, already in his 50s. She watched from afar because, in those days, children were not allowed to be present while adults talked, or in this case, negotiated.

But what was this man looking to buy? It wasn't land, it wasn't cattle. It was something more human—better said, someone.

Yes, you guessed it correctly. This man wanted to buy Ager. That unexpected visit would change Ager's life forever. A few days later, her parents called her in and asked her... I'm laughing at the word I just wrote—"asked her." No, it wasn't like that. They ordered her to pack her things the following week because she had to go live with that man she didn't know. Not as his daughter but as his wife.

The first thing we think when we read this is the first thing I said when I heard this sad story: "If it had been me, I wouldn't have done it; I wouldn't have obeyed my parents; I would have run away from home." But as the years passed, I realized that every era has its stories and every situation has its mysteries.

I really don't know if it's because women are more independent now or if people are more understanding of others' pain.
Back then, most of the elders in the villages thought alike. There wasn't as much technology as there is now, and there weren't institutions that protected minors. It was a time with its own advantages and disadvantages. If she had decided not to obey, where would she go? That's what she thought.

While her parents talked to her, something broke inside her, something that would take many years to mend. Those days, she didn't want to go out to play anymore; she had no appetite and didn't want to talk to anyone. She just wanted to understand what was happening to her. When Saturday came, she had to go with that man who could have been her grandfather. And although that man wasn't one of those brutal types, that moment marked her life forever. She felt so many things: disgust, shame, and pain. She felt pain because her mother hadn't understood her, hadn't listened to her. Well, maybe because her mother had gone through the same thing, maybe because she thought it wasn't as difficult as it seemed.

Her mother didn't know any other way to handle things. Maybe she no longer had feelings, or if she did, she didn't want to express them to avoid more suffering. Ager had no escape from that life her parents had chosen for her. She started down that path without anyone telling her the damage it would cause her. Before this happened, she was a cheerful, innocent, happy, friendly, sincere young girl, and one could almost say she enjoyed talking about God.

She had other dreams. She had dreamed of many things. She had dreamed just like you and I once did.
She thought about finishing a career; she wanted to be a doctor, meet a good young man around her age, get married, and have children. All those dreams vanished like smoke, without her planning it, she had to abandon them. In this sad situation, she couldn't live long because that man wouldn't let her go anywhere. At first, she thought about committing suicide, but someone had talked to her about God, and she knew that wasn't what God wanted for her.

One day, after a few months, a light dawned on her, and in her mind she devised a small plan. Without phone calls, without the internet, without letters to let anyone know she was coming. She thought of going to her aunt who lived in the city.

And so she did. One day when the man had gone out to take care of some business in town, she asked him to buy something that would take her with him, and he agreed. She was so disoriented that that trip seemed like hours to her when it was only about 15 minutes.

Already in town, a bit scared, she put on makeup as best she could to look older. She bought her ticket and left for the city, a two-hour journey, during which she cried, bitter like a woman who had lost everything. Luckily, she knew her aunt's address. And luckily, and thanks to the time period, it took a few days for her parents to find out where she was.

Her aunt asked few questions, as she was one of the few people of that time who understood young people. Her aunt knew what she had been through and didn't leave her alone. She let her cry as much as she wanted, and so a few days passed.

One early morning, a man's voice was heard in her aunt's living room. It was the voice of her older brother, who had come for Ager. Ager was very afraid, but she knew one thing: she would never see that old man again.

She explained to her brother, and much to his reluctance, he left, and her aunt took care of Ager. Those few months Ager had lived with that man marked her for life. She was never the same. She was never again the young girl who brought joy to everyone. Something had happened to her laughter. Her dreams had been shattered. How sad, don't you think? How could Ager forget what she had lived through? How could she forgive her parents? How could she return to the place of her dreams when she didn't know the way back?

She wanted to forget, but you and I know it's not that easy

to achieve. And although time passed, she was marked for life. In the 1980s, she met Jesus, but even so, she remained a woman embittered by the pain of the past, because she always thought her life should have been different, that she should have been a great doctor.

Ager was trapped by her pain. God had a plan for Ager's life that, although it was brutally interrupted by that sad situation, she could have overcome it with God's help, if she had allowed it. She never managed to overcome that past and lived in bitterness until the day she died. God is willing to turn our pain into joy. He is willing to bring joy where there is pain. God wants us to learn to trust in Him. He wants us to know that He wants to set the brokenhearted free.

Ager never gave God a chance to show her the difference between the joy of the world and the joy in Him. Will you? Will you allow God to change your life? She shut herself off and closed the opportunity to love again. She was not happy with the man God gave her, because the memory of that old man kept coming back to her over and over again.

She never believed in anyone again, did not enjoy her daughters—God blessed her with two beautiful girls—but she never realized this wonderful gift because she was always thinking that others were not sincere with her, as the memory of that betrayal was always on her mind. She did not allow herself to be healed by God. She did not enjoy what she had, suffering for what she had lost.

At the end of her days, she let herself die at only 34 years of age. She had a terminal illness that, if treated in time, might have allowed her to raise her daughters, but she could not because Ager no longer wanted to trust anyone else. Ager remained silent without seeking treatment, until one day her husband discovered her, but unfortunately, it was too late, and shortly afterward she died.

I saw her cry because she did not want to die and leave her young daughters orphaned, but she should not have died that way. She denied herself the opportunity to believe in people again, and by not trusting her husband, she chose to let herself die without doing anything.

She was so young and did not deserve to die; I know that, but we also know that there are people who deny themselves the chance to start over. Ager had the opportunity to live again; God had given her enough reasons to feel happy, but she chose to cry over what she did not have and what she had lived through.

Ager did not want to forgive; she was filled with hatred and bitterness, not only towards her parents but also towards everyone around her. She could not only not love anyone, but she also did not let anyone love her. She refused to believe in love and preferred to die a prisoner of herself.

Reflect.

This is one of the stories from my memory that has touched my heart the most. I hope that the Holy Spirit has touched your heart while you were reading. It is my heart's desire that you understand that God wants to heal hearts that have been damaged. He has a remedy; He has medicine for you.

No matter how hard or sad your story is, there is someone who wants to change the hue of your life's picture. He wants to add color where there is only darkness. Give Him the opportunity to make art with your life. I cannot change lives; I cannot create new things (in a spiritual sense), but God can if you truly believe and allow Him to make His masterpiece with you.

Will you let Him work with you? If your heart is wounded, then you need God's help to heal you because if not, you will hurt others, even if you don't want to, and you will be surrounded by problems caused by the same pain you have in your heart.

You will see ghosts where there are none, you will not believe in anyone, you will think that no one loves you, when in reality, you are the one who has not opened yourself to enjoy all the wonderful people God has placed around you.

Open your eyes and look around, and you will realize that there will always be someone who loves you, someone who is waiting for you, someone who would like to understand you. But it's not always easy; you yourself must recognize that sometimes you don't even know what's going on with you.

It's time to stop blaming others for our misfortunes and give others the chance to live alongside us. Yes, to live, because the aim of this feeling of unlove, which does not come from God, is to drive you away from everyone who loves you.

It will not always be easy to open your heart. But it's worth trying.

Frustration arises as a consequence of not fulfilling your dreams. It comes from someone having damaged your plans, not because you wanted it, but because circumstances dictated it. But happiness comes as a result of the decision to be happy.

No one else but you is responsible for feeling happy. Happiness is not a stable state or a matter of social status; it is a daily decision.

CHAPTER 5

There are times when a woman cries over her past. She cries because there is a past behind her, she cries because there are those who accuse her and because, although she wishes to change her life and forget what has happened, her life will never be the same with this past, which is a source of shame for her.

This, in turn, becomes a feeling of guilt. Who knows this better than Liz?

Dominated by Passion

Liz is our next character. Liz was not a good wife. She didn't know how to be one; although she had tried for a couple of years, she had not succeeded.

That morning, Liz had gotten up like every other morning. While she was bathing, she thought about Luis. He had told her that he loved her. She could still feel his touches on her body, and the taste of his kisses was fresh in her mouth.

Her thoughts were interrupted by a tormenting thought. She felt ashamed of her relationship with Luis. She felt that what she was doing was wrong. For a moment, she thought she should leave that man who made her unfaithful. Suddenly, she realized she was trapped by passion—the passion that Luis aroused in her.

A few tears ran down her wet cheek, and she sighed without speaking. She heard an unusual whistle. Liz knew it was that man who drove her crazy; for a moment, she thought about ignoring him and not responding to his call. But how could she?

Luis arrived, kissed her, and began to tell her that he loved her. Liz tried to say something, but he took her in his arms and kissed her. He kissed her as if it were the last kiss.

Liz finds herself trapped in his arms, clinging to a passion she cannot control. Or perhaps she does not want to? What do you think?

Suddenly, voices are heard in the living room. Liz thinks it's her husband who has returned from his trip. She realizes it is not her husband, but other people who have arrived at the house. She tries to go see who has arrived, but Luis doesn't let her.

She thinks to herself that it is like other times. "I'll let the servants attend to them; they think I am asleep," Liz thinks. She follows her thoughts and succumbs to her body, which does not want to part from her man.

She surrenders in his arms, and they end up consummating their passion.

Luis is in a hurry because he has to work, so he starts getting dressed. But she does not want him to leave, and she gets out of bed wrapped in her sheet and covers him with her naked body, trying to seduce him as she has done before.

He tells her no, and while they are talking, a couple of men with familiar faces enter the room. They are the church officials, the leaders who judge the people, and they have caught her without clothes and in the arms of a man who is not her husband.

She manages to put on a nightgown and tries to explain what is happening, while Luis, without saying a word, runs out of the room. The men seem indifferent to Luis's escape, as if he does not concern them.

"Adulteress, we will kill you," says one of the chief members of the Sanhedrin.

When they took her to Caiaphas, he had a better idea: to bring her to Jesus.

Liz felt immense shame. She was devastated as she had not even been allowed to get dressed. She felt ruined not only because she was going to be killed but also because Luis had left her alone at the moment she needed him the most.

Now Liz would no longer be called by her name but rather as "the adulteress."
They brought her to Jesus, but He did not condemn her. No, He asked, "Where are those who accuse you?"
Jesus made her understand that everyone had a very clear reason not to accuse her. They too were sinners. Jesus wanted to tell Liz not to embrace the condemnation of people, not to accept that they would kill her, and that all sins before Him are the same. She needed to release her guilt because no one could accuse her before Him.

He forgave her. But He said, "Go and sin no more," as if to say: "I forgive you, but value this forgiveness. Go and be different, go and do not be called 'the adulteress,' but rather 'the forgiven, the changed.'" This is the message of our Lord: "Be different."

What does this mean? That I cannot change my past, but I can change my present.

Reflection

The word "passion" comes from the Greek word "pathos," which appears in the plural in Romans 1:26 and Colossians 3:5. These verses denote the disordered emotions or feelings of unredeemed human nature that must be subjected to the governance of the Holy Spirit.

The verb derived from the same root "pathos" means "sufferings."

This clearly explains why women who give free rein to their feelings or who are caught up in passion, just like this woman who is none other than the adulteress, always end up trapped in deep pain.

This results from the root cause, which is disordered passion towards sex.

According to the law, adultery deserved the death penalty, but the accused had to be caught in the act and also had the right to a trial, with certain procedures agreed upon to establish their guilt or innocence. This can be seen in Numbers 5:11-31.

The adulteress was not subjected to any trial but was used by the authorities to set a trap for Jesus.

In Mosaic law, when King David repented of his sin of adultery, God forgave him (2 Samuel 11:2-5 and Psalm 51:1,2).

In the New Testament, the Lord Jesus declares that adultery is not only committed through the act itself but also through looking and coveting, implying that the desire for it, like all sin that originates in the heart, is also a sin.

The adulterous woman, as the Bible calls her, is known for her sin. How sad it is to be known for what we do, and even worse when what we have done is shameful.

I have named her Liz to give this character, whom God wants us to know, a name and to identify her with women today. Liz wanted to be a good wife; she wanted to love her husband. But despite trying for years, she fell into infidelity and was caught up in passion—the passion of youth. She allowed herself to be seduced by the lies that a man seeking adventures is capable of telling.

We learn that:

- *It is not enough to be religious.*
- *It is not enough to want to be good, as this will not help us with marital problems.*
- *We must seek God.*
- *We need to pray more.*
- *Seek a friend, and note that I said "friend," meaning it should be a woman because otherwise, Satan can deceive you and trap you in temptation.*
- *Seek advice, but not from immature young women who just want to "enjoy their lives" or their youth as they put it.*

- You should seek women who are examples through their lives.

The adulterous woman, if she had not encountered Jesus, would surely have died. But even if we bring this story to our time and culture, even though there is no death penalty for adultery, the internal experience of a woman who falls into adultery is almost the same.

The shame of what she has done prevents her from living, and this manifests in different ways. She might shut herself away and never forgive herself, sometimes even as a Christian. But she might also take a wrong path and fall into sexual depravity, as Satan will make her believe that she is already so tainted that nothing she does will change that.

Do not remain crying over your misfortune, as even if you cannot see it, there is always something that can be done. It is never too late if you want to change your life. Sincerity with God will help you move forward. God knows your needs and has always wanted to help you. Take the hand He is offering you today and listen to His voice saying, "I do not condemn you; go and sin no more."

In the New Testament, the Lord Jesus declares that adultery is not only committed through the act itself but also through looking and coveting, implying that the desire for it, like all sin that originates in the heart, is also a sin.

The adulterous woman, as the Bible calls her, is known for her sin. How sad it is to be known for what we do, and even worse when what we have done is shameful.

I have named her Liz to give this character, whom God wants us to know, a name and to identify her with women today. Liz wanted to be a good wife; she wanted to love her husband. But despite trying for years, she fell into infidelity and was caught up in passion—the passion of youth. She allowed herself to be seduced by the lies that a man seeking adventures is capable of telling.

We learn that:

- *It is not enough to be religious.*
- *It is not enough to want to be good, as this will not help us with marital problems.*
- *We must seek God.*
- *We need to pray more.*
- *Seek a friend, and note that I said "friend," meaning it should be a woman because otherwise, Satan can deceive you and trap you in temptation.*
- *Seek advice, but not from immature young women who just want to "enjoy their lives" or their youth as they put it.*
- *You should seek women who are examples through their lives.*

The adulterous woman, if she had not encountered Jesus, would surely have died. But even if we bring this story to our time and culture, even though there is no death penalty for adultery, the internal experience of a woman who falls into adultery is almost the same.

The shame of what she has done prevents her from living, and this manifests in different ways. She might shut herself away and never forgive herself, sometimes even as a Christian. But she might also take a wrong path and fall into sexual depravity, as Satan will make her believe that she is already so tainted that nothing she does will change that.

Do not remain crying over your misfortune, as even if you cannot see it, there is always something that can be done. It is never too late if you want to change your life. Sincerity with God will help you move forward. God knows your needs and has always wanted to help you. Take the hand He is offering you today and listen to His voice saying, "I do not condemn you; go and sin no more."

CHAPTER 6

Nostalgia for the Past?

The past is a shadow. Is it something that no longer exists? I don't think so. Sometimes it's a smile that is no longer there. It's a friend we will never see again. Sometimes the past is sad, and other times it's joyful.

If we could go back to the past, how many things would we change? I don't think any. I think we might end up repeating the same things that have happened before, making the same mistakes, but unfortunately, we think differently.

For this reason, I believe that God has established that man lives only once because He does not want man to live the same thing twice. I wonder: Doesn't the same thing happen day after day, year after year, century after century? Aren't the events essentially the same?

Maybe not with the same people, but certainly with a human being just like you and me. The same repeated lies, the same abuses, the same anger repeated over and over.

We may change fashion or hairstyles, but under the sun, the same things keep happening.

The past should help us reflect on the falls of others. The wounds of our relatives should teach us that there is something in human beings that is not right.

But what is not right? Who taught us that a painting should be hung on the wall? Why not place it on the floor? Who taught us that we should eat with utensils and on a table? Who taught us that we should have this and use that?

I believe life itself. Life has taken care of teaching those who didn't know how things work in this world we live in. We have accepted its suggestions without complaint, and there are moments when we feel unhappy because we don't have everything that life has suggested to everyone.

Is there someone in this highly technological world who can truly live without what our times suggest? It seems not; it's unfortunate, but we all want to be on the same level.

Many of us come from "dysfunctional" families, as my friend psychology would say. Many of us carry a past that does not belong to us, and live with customs we have adopted as our own without anyone asking us what we wanted to choose; we have chosen without having our own decision-making power.

Think for a moment about something you have experienced, that someone else chose for you without asking you anything.

We have been suggested many things, even what we should eat. Our parents received this from their parents, we received it from them, and our children will receive it from us. Many have begun their lives without realizing that their steps have been suggested by others. It seems that no one really wants to be different. Everyone wants to do the same things, so no one feels sad.

Our past is important, not for us to live in it, but for us to learn from it. God's desire in creating a new day every 24 hours was to suggest that He wanted us to experience new things.

God's desire is that you do not live a life of learned customs. He wants you to learn to choose based on your own convictions. If it were otherwise, He would have created us without the power of choice. But thanks to Him, every human being can choose whom they want to serve. Have you chosen Him? Or have you been suggested someone you should choose?

We have the capacity to decide what we want to do with our lives, and we cannot blame anyone else. If you made a mistake yesterday because you didn't know or because someone else made the choice for you, remember that God has created new days. Without any problems, you can start a new path today. I know that if you want to, God will help you start again.

Jesus is willing to do for you what He did for someone else yesterday. The miracle you need is not impossible if you truly believe it! If so, say Amen.

CHAPTER 7

The story you are about to read is about a woman who repeatedly tried to change her life, who longed to be loved and believed that with each new husband she would achieve what she had dreamed of since childhood. However, for reasons unknown, her dreams turned into her worst nightmare—a never-satisfied emptiness.

Iris was a very beautiful young woman. She had stunning eyes, long black hair that reached almost to her waist, and a complexion that was neither too dark nor too light. She was a light brown-skinned woman, tall, and with such a slender figure that one could say it was almost perfect, modesty aside.

Iris was beautiful, from a good family, young, but she did not know Jesus, our Savior. Thus, Iris was planning her future alone and without a good guide. She did not know, although she believed she had everything to gain because she was beautiful and wealthy.

Iris started her journey at a very young age. She fell in love with a neighbor, who also fell in love with her. They decided to marry, even though Iris thought it was still too soon to talk about marriage. José wanted to marry her because he was afraid she might regret marrying him. José did not consider himself very attractive; he was short and somewhat overweight, which made him feel insecure about Iris's love.

They got married, and at first, everything was very nice. Iris was happy and felt like the happiest woman in the world. This happiness lasted very little, as José was not a man of means like her, and he did not have the luxuries she was accustomed to. Iris did not know how to cook, iron, or do laundry—basically, she did not know how to run a household.

She decided to go to her parents' house and spend the day there, thus avoiding the discomfort of their small apartment and bringing food to her husband at night. She thought that with this brilliant idea, all her problems were solved. But the truth was that this was her idea, not José's. José felt humiliated by this idea; he felt that she did not love him, that he was too insignificant for her, which caused him growing anger and jealousy. Iris did not know this, as José was very quiet and, moreover, was always exhausted from his hard work. He had accepted to work extra hours in hopes of saving money to find a bigger house where Iris would feel more comfortable.

The problems worsened with the extra hours. José was always very irritable due to lack of sleep, and the little time he spent with Iris, he was always very tired. This marriage lasted a year and a couple of months because José, after a heated argument, did not return home and decided to leave Iris without any explanation.

Iris was devastated for a few months as she could not understand what she had done wrong or where she had made a mistake.

After this, four months later, she ran into a high school friend she had not seen for about three years by chance. He invited her out, and she accepted. Iris, without realizing it, began to fall in love with Martín, and they decided to live together. But two months later, on a Saturday at 10 a.m., a young pregnant woman showed up looking for Martín. She was not like Iris; she was poor and very humble. Upon realizing that Iris was living with Martín, she decided to leave without saying a word. Iris realized she had made a serious mistake by rushing to live with Martín, so this time she was not willing to be left behind and packed her things, wrote a small note, and left.

At this point, Iris began to suffer from depression. She could not understand why these things were happening to her, and she felt embarrassed by her neighbors, as many believed she was the problem. Iris decided not to believe in love again.

A few years passed, and a friend invited her to a party, and she decided to go. It was a Sunday night, almost 11 p.m., when a very attractive young man arrived at the party. She had decided to leave, but her friend wanted to introduce her to Carlos. Carlos was very handsome and knew it; he was a wealthy and somewhat arrogant young man, about Iris's age and not yet 30. When they were introduced, Carlos was captivated by Iris's beauty and invited her to dance. She refused and left.

Iris was tired, not only from the party but also from her own life. She was still very young but felt as if she had lived a lot. She did not want to start another relationship with anyone; she was determined to wait for the man of her life.

On Monday, around 4 p.m., she received a large bouquet of orchids. She did not know who had sent them, but she had never received such a large and beautiful bouquet before. Along with the flowers was a small note that read, "Your beauty surpasses these flowers." It did not say who had sent them, but Iris felt very flattered. It had been a long time since anyone had called her beautiful; she could not remember the last time.

On the back of the card was something written that she had not noticed: "If you want, we can meet tonight. I will be waiting for you," followed by an address.

Iris felt a bit scared but decided to go to the meeting, asking her friend Laura to accompany her, which she did. When they arrived at the restaurant where they were meeting, Carlos was there with more flowers in hand.

Laura understood that she was unnecessary and, despite Iris's request not to leave, she decided to go, knowing her friend needed a companion, according to Laura.

After that evening, Carlos made Iris believe he was a true gentleman, different from others. He wanted to win her over, and this was not a problem for him, as he was used to seducing women. He had done it many times before and had rarely failed. With Iris, it was a bit different because he could not impress her with his money or his looks, as she was also beautiful and might even surpass him in beauty.

Weeks passed, and Carlos put all his effort into what he called "his new conquest," as he told his friends. He sent orchids, called her every night, and visited her when she did not want to go out. He made her believe he truly loved her, until one night on a beach at a camp, Iris believed in his promises of love and decided to give herself another chance in love, as her friend Laura had advised.

Soon, Iris became Carlos's wife.

Carlos was different from her first husband; he didn't have

to work, and he had a mansion even larger than Iris's parents'. He was a man of her own class. He thought like her, and they had the same friends. All of Iris's friends were happy with this relationship, but something inside her told her that Carlos was not what he seemed. She didn't feel secure, and every time Carlos went out with his friends, she knew something could happen.

Their relationship lasted 8 months. Iris suspected Carlos was cheating on her, and she was right. One day, her friend Laura invited her out for a meal, and she accepted. They went to a restaurant that Laura frequented, and Iris had the shock of her life when she found Carlos with another woman.

It was not so hard for her, as she had decided not to give her heart to someone as cold as Carlos. They did not argue, and although Carlos wanted to continue with her, Iris did not want to live in the hypocrisy of a man who did not love her. She went back home again, this time not like the others. There was no drama of tears or manifested depression; although her parents wanted to discuss the matter, she decided not to talk about her life anymore. She didn't even want to talk to Laura, who knew about it but hadn't told her.

Iris began visiting an institution that helped young people with problems, and she had started having issues with alcohol and insomnia due to depression. Her parents had a friend who worked with people with problems, and Iris began attending that place. She improved a lot, remembered that she liked painting, and spent her time on that.

One day at the center, she noticed a man she had known since childhood. He treated her so well, understood her, knew what she felt and thought. This man was Felipe. She had known him since she was a child. He had watched her grow up, and she had played with his children since Felipe was a personal friend of Iris's father.

Felipe was a 53-year-old man, but despite his age, he was very elegant and yet simple, a calm and homely man. He had been widowed for about 8 years and had not remarried. He had little time for love; he had been married for 20 years to a wonderful woman, and together they had 3 children—2 sons and a daughter, who was Laura, her friend.

She decided to paint him in silence, and as she painted, she fell more in love with him each day. One day, Laura was celebrating her birthday and they had a party. At the end of the party, Iris decided to provoke Felipe, asking him to drive her home because she felt unwell, which was a lie.

On the way home, Iris gave him the painting she had made of him. He found it a very nice gesture. They stopped at a spot to view the painting, which was still a scroll without a frame. When they got out of the car in front of a hill overlooking the city, she confessed her feelings for him. He was very surprised and said nothing; she kissed him without saying a word.

Iris's passion drove Felipe wild, and that very night they began a secret relationship, not because she wanted to, but because Felipe felt embarrassed about his children and Iris's parents. They always met alone in an apartment that he had, which belonged to a son who was traveling. Nobody suspected they were lovers. They maintained this relationship for 3 years.

One day, Felipe fell ill and could not return to work; he had terminal cancer, and the doctors gave no assurance of recovery. Despite the surgeries and chemotherapy, Felipe died after three months, leaving Iris in the darkest depression. Felipe was the only man she had truly loved, and despite no one understanding her situation, she tried to commit suicide a couple of times until her parents suggested she go on a trip. She agreed and left.

Thus, Iris began a new life away from her parents. Two years later, she decided to return to where her parents lived, but this time she looked for an apartment and began living alone. She started a new life, and one day at a party, she met a man who seduced her, and she went with him to a hotel.

A few days later, Iris visited an old friend, María, and to her surprise, when María introduced her husband, it was Pedro—the same man she had met at the party last month. She left immediately, and Pedro offered to drive her home. It was then that he told her he no longer wanted-ed María.

Iris continued seeing Pedro from time to time until one day she met a man who shared his entire life with her. He asked about her husband, and she told him she was not married. This man was different; he revealed things to her that even her friends didn't know. This man was Jesus, who changed her and made her realize that the void she had been trying to fill with men could only be filled with God.

Jesus made her understand that she needed an encounter with Him to quench the thirst she had felt for years. For years, she had tried to understand why no one could fulfill her and why she wasn't happy.

She went and called her parents, her friends, and told everyone that she had met a man and this is what happened.

Iris: "I have met a man."
Her father responded: "Another one? My daughter, I think it's better not to get your hopes up too much."
Iris: "I'm talking about a wonderful man who told me my whole life."
Laura: "But Iris, remember that everyone in town talks about your story. There is no one who doesn't know everything that has happened to you."
Iris: "But this man is a prophet. I think you should know him."
Iris's mother: "To know your life, you don't have to be a prophet."

That's when Iris realized she had to tell the truth, no matter how hard it was, if she wanted them to know that man called Jesus.

There was a moment of silence and a sigh was heard. Iris, with a worried look, looked at everyone and began to speak again.

Iris: "Mom, Dad, siblings, and friends, especially you, Laura and María."

Pedro, who was also there, realized Iris was about to speak and stood up, saying, "You've gone crazy; think about the consequences," and left.

Iris continued: "Forgive me. For more than three years, I was Felipe's mistress, and we were happy. He never wanted it to be known because he felt ashamed with you and with you, Laura, and your siblings. Forgive me, Laura. María, until yesterday, I was your husband's mistress, but I don't want to be the same anymore. I want to change my life and live without deceit or lies.

I'm sorry. I know that this man is a man of God. If you want, you can come tomorrow to meet him, as he will be here."

I don't know what happened after that meeting, but they believed in Jesus because Iris chose to tell the truth to everyone and live without masks.

Reflection

This story shows us that to change our lives, we cannot do it alone but with the help of our Lord, who can give us to drink from that water.

This story is not just about the sin of fornication but also about a feeling that harms: the feeling of dissatisfaction. It is a feeling produced by the lack of the Spirit of God in people, aimed at making the person realize they need to seek Him.

This feeling will manifest in different ways. It will make you an unstable person, not only in marriage but in anything you start. It will make you feel incomplete in everything, meaning you will feel that something is missing even if you laugh, and even if you try to fill yourself with things from this world, you won't succeed.

The story of the Samaritan woman is fascinating, not only because it teaches us how to deal with problems with people of different customs, cultures, or races. It is a story that shows us that Jesus is interested in our personal lives and that this gospel means change, not only outwardly but inwardly.

The Samaritan woman encountered Christ, and He gave her a lesson that I believe is also for us today. She had an inner void that she tried to fill with different men. She needed to be loved, just like all women, as this is one of a woman's needs. This need drives them to make mistakes without considering the consequences.

She didn't understand that religion couldn't help her, that a man couldn't quench the thirst she had, a thirst that wasn't for water.

Today, we live in a different time than that era. Some of us live in continents with cultures different from that of this woman. But a woman's needs transcend cultures and customs. No matter the culture, if you are a woman, you will have the same needs, and this will lead you to fall if your void is not filled with the Holy Spirit and if your thirst is not quenched by the water that only Jesus can offer.

The story of this woman is evidence that God is interested in changing lives, regardless of how sinful they may be, the failures they have had, or the past they have lived. He is interested in you, not in your past, but in what you, as a person, are worth. Most importantly, He wants you to be honest so that He can fill you.

When the woman asked Jesus for water, He told her, "Go and call your husband." She replied, "I have no husband," trying to bypass her past. Jesus revealed her life to her, helping us understand that to drink from the water that gives eternal life, we cannot hide our sins. He wants to change you and do something new with you, but you need to be honest with God and remove the "good girl" mask before Him.

Allow yourself to be changed by the power of our God, and surrender to Him with a sincere heart. Jesus told the woman that if she knew the "gift of God," she would ask Him for water. I invite you to do as the Samaritan woman did and ask the Master for water.

I invite you to drink from that water, and you will see that you will never feel thirsty again. What thirst? You won't feel like nothing fills you because God Himself will satisfy that inner void that can only be filled by Him.

CHAPTER 8

The past can be difficult for some people, especially for those who have to make decisions in their present that will affect their future. But the big question is, what can I do about my past?

What can a person who has to start over do? What should they do to move forward with their life, especially when this past that is still part of their present is significant? Many people never manage to change their lives because they are unable to start a new present completely separate from their past.

Decisions that affect your present and future.

The story we will see next is about a woman who could not start anew, even though she wanted to try.

Joaida is a woman of nearly 45 years old. She has never traveled and has never lived in any country other than the one she was born in. Joaida is a woman who does not know God. She has never served Him and has only heard her husband speak of Him a few times.

Her husband is very God-fearing. He teaches their two daughters that they should fear this God whom Joaida does not know. Joaida and her family have lived their entire lives in this country. This country is in serious trouble with the God she does not know.

Joaida's parents died here, her siblings live here, and her daughters were born here. Everything related to her is tied to this country. This will be her last night in the land that saw her birth. From her bedroom window, she is watching her last sunset.

Tears run down her cheeks as she packs her bags. She is trying to be strong, as she does not want her two daughters to know that she is completely broken. She has packed sandals, shoes, clothes, and above all, many memories, gifts given to her on special occasions.

While packing, she finds the dress she wore on her wedding day; it is a bit small because she was thinner when she got married. She begins to remember that day, and when she sees in the old closet the first shoe her first daughter ever wore, Joaida realizes that this change would not be as easy as her husband had said. She begins to wonder how she could pack the things that are not visible.

She starts to cry silently, not because she has to start over, not because she will lose her friends, but because her soul remains in that place. She cries because part of her is staying behind, and she cannot pack it into the suitcase she has.

How could she leave that place and lose part of her life without feeling the pain of the loss?

It was the moment of truth. She had to leave this place, not by her will, but to save her life, and she did not know how to do this. She knew that Sodom would be destroyed by morning.

That night she did not sleep but waited for her last dawn. Although her body was tired, she wanted to enjoy the last sun and see the new dawn of a new day.

Lot, her husband, had no trouble packing. He was used to moving frequently, and this time, he knew he had no choice, as the decision was not his but rather that the city would be destroyed by God. Lot knew God and understood that it was best for him and his family to obey the command given by the angels.

Lot tried to help his wife understand, but she was not in a position to comprehend. She was already disturbed, and her mind could only think of what she was leaving behind. In other words, Joaida could only think of her past; she thought she could not continue living without her customs.

When the new day arrived, Lot and his family were forced by the angels to leave Sodom. Joaida took her bags and left with her husband and two daughters for an unknown place.

She felt empty, alone, sad, broken, and felt as if her life was left behind in Sodom. And I believe that she left with her body from Sodom, but her heart stayed. She made her best effort to obey. She obeyed the command to leave, obeyed the urgency of the angels; that is, she left just in time. But there was one command she could not obey, even though she tried, and that was not to look back. She could not avoid looking back because her soul and heart were behind. She had left her soul in Sodom, and for this reason, on the way to safety, she could not go on. She could not leave her nation alone; she wanted to die among its ruins. She did not want to continue living in something different and new. She did not want to leave Sodom as part of her past; for her, it was easier to not move forward and die with Sodom than to start a new life.

As she was about to escape, she looked back and became a pillar of salt.

What a sad end! She turned into a pillar of salt, but she was already like that inside; her heart no longer felt, nor did her soul.

What happened to Joaida, as we have called her, was that her spiritual condition became visible. Although she left Sodom with her body, her heart was far from the salvation that God had provided for them.

Where is your heart? Is it in the place of salvation that God has provided for you, or is it in the place from which God has taken or wants to take you?

Reflection.

What is a decision? A decision is when something is decided. Now, what does it mean to decide? According to the Encarta Encyclopedia, it means to "resolve a difficulty. Formulate a definitive judgment. Move the will to reach a determination."

If we analyze Lot's wife's situation, we will realize that she never decided to leave Sodom. Let's look at a few points:

She did not make a judgment about the situation to realize that she truly needed to leave with determination.
She did not move her will in the supposed decision to leave Sodom.
She did not make a determination on her own.

The problem when we do not make the right decisions is that, in reality, we have not moved our will in the direction that is truly beneficial for us. Joaida was aware that her nation was wicked; she knew that her people were cruel and rebellious against God. But how could she leave her beloved nation? She let her emotions overpower her reason.

She had tried to convince her childhood friends to leave that life, but they called her crazy. Joaida, like many people, could not detach herself from her past, which is a problem many people today face, ordinary people like you and me.

I cannot tell you that starting over has never been easy, nor will it ever be. But it is important that we learn from the story of Lot's wife and her failure to face the reality of having to leave the past, which never truly became her past because she did not want to change her life.

God was giving her an opportunity to start anew, just as He may be offering you in your life. God wanted to save her, and for this reason, He provided a way for her and her family to escape the wrath of God. She obeyed and began to walk the path of salvation, though only with her body, because her soul and heart (her emotions) had not yet left that place of perdition called Sodom.

The path she walked was because she was being led. But even though her eyes were not crying at that moment, her tears had never ceased, for her heart was broken and she was crying inside.

She felt such immense pain that, even if she wanted to, she couldn't explain to anyone what she was feeling. Could you explain it? When something makes you cry, can you identify what you feel and what is happening to you? Can you overcome it?

There are times when we cannot do what we need to do because our feelings hold us back, or maybe we just don't want to. Our soul may resist doing what is right, and if what is right is starting a new life in God, in the salvation He has provided for us, we need to be strong, overcome our pain and feelings, and make the right decision.

Perhaps your story is different from Joaida's; perhaps you do not live in a city called Sodom.

Your Sodom might be:

- *A man who is not right for you, whom you need to leave.*
- *A person you need to forgive.*
- *A toxic friend or family member you need to distance yourself from.*
- *A place you need to stop frequenting.*
- *A habit you need to set aside and say no to, disrupting your routine, breaking the custom that prevents you from being flexible with God, and looking forward instead of turning into a pillar of salt.*

What does this mean? It means that God has called us to be salt, but not a pile of salt that is useless because it is stagnant and cannot be moved from its current state. The spiritual state that helps us grow is one that allows us to be sensitive to God's changes through the gentle voice of His precious Spirit within us. Glory to God!

Stagnation will result in defeat after defeat in our lives and is a visible sign that we have emotional problems. We must be open to God changing our past and present into the precious future He has prepared for us.

When making decisions, do not be negligent. Take seriously everything related to your spiritual future. Do not be weak in leaving Sodom. I believe you understand the spiritual language that symbolizes your Sodom.

CHAPTER 9

Changed Behind the Wall

It is a morning in 1999. Everything seems normal in my home. I smell its distinctive aroma, the scent of freshly brewed coffee, which reminds me of my grandmother Aurora, who is no longer with me. The green furniture I had reupholstered looks great in my modest house. I'm sitting at the dining table in front of a painting that captured my attention at first sight. I was struck by it, though I didn't know why. I was captivated by the nature that emanated from it—the majestic green, the lake running through a small hut nestled between the mountains, and the wild, giant pine that the size of the painting could not fully capture. Thinking about it, I'm not really sure what specifically drew my admiration to this painting.

Perhaps it was the blue sky intertwining with a mountain that seemed to want to become part of the sky. That's how I see it. Although there are two other mountains in the landscape blending into all the green, my eyes can only focus on one. The same goes for the pines; there are many of them, of all sizes, part of the same scene, but despite their number, only one caught my attention. It is bigger than the painting, taller than the mountains, taller than the other pines surrounding it, and I am certain that the painter wanted to highlight that giant pine, and I think he succeeded.

At that moment, it came to my mind that last night the Lord spoke to me. He made me see two paintings reflecting scenes from my life. There were two paintings that seemed identical but were not. In one of the paintings, there was a painter who was not painting but was in front of one of the paintings trying to do something with it. Over time, that painter, who was the Lord, began to change the color of one of the paintings. The painting He was working on had a lot of color and brightness. Although it was not finished, it was clear that there was a marked difference between the painting that God's finger was repairing and the one with only shadows, reflecting pain and sadness.

Seeing this confused me for a moment, and then I heard the voice of the great painter saying to me: "If you let me, I can change your life. If you let me, I can add color to your life and turn your pain into joy." At that moment, I understood that the Lord was telling me that sometimes I didn't let Him work as He wanted, and that what I was doing was ruining myself by not wanting to change and start anew.

I thought about Rahab, as I have been meditating a lot on the woman of Lot lately and wondered why she didn't want to start anew. I found that there were people in the Bible who decided to leave everything behind and start afresh, even though they never thought they could catch the attention of this great painter, but they did. I have been asking myself: How did they do it?

So today, I am going to visit my friend Rahab to see if she can tell me something about it.

It's 5 in the afternoon, and I have arrived at my friend's house. After we chatted for a while, she told me her story.

Here's what my friend Rahab told me:

"I was trapped in that city with no way out. I felt sad because I knew they would defeat us. I was absolutely sure they would win; I don't know why, but for some strange reason, I felt it in my heart. A woman I met told me that the people behind the wall were the people of a very powerful God, a God who had never lost a battle. The fear of God had fallen over my entire nation, and all we heard was talk of the warriors of Israel."

Rahab: "Would you like more coffee?"

Me: "Yes, thank you. And keep telling me what you did to

save yourself."

Rahab: "Well, I'll tell you that at night I couldn't sleep, and I was considering closing the business."

Me: "What business?"

Rahab: "Don't you know I had a dating business, a bar where pleasure was sold to men."

Rahab continued telling me.

I wondered what I would live on if I closed the business. A few days passed, and I decided to take the risk and talk to one of those from the enemy's town. Every day, I sat at the entrance of the wall waiting.

On the third day, I saw some rather unusual men entering the city. If anyone knew the men from that city, it was me. I approached to offer them my services, but they seemed uninterested. I asked them where they were from and what they were looking for, but they didn't answer. I noticed they spoke with a somewhat strange accent, which revealed them as foreigners. There were guards around, and those men became a little nervous.

At that moment, I realized they were spies, and I wanted to tell them what I wanted, but there were guards nearby, so I pretended they were my clients and quickly took them to my establishment.

When we arrived at the bar, it hadn't yet closed. There were a few customers, including some of the king's guards, who were among my best clients. One of the spies wanted to eat but refused what we offered, so one of the king's guards hurried to the royal palace to inform the king. Just like me, he had also realized that these men were spies.

I closed the bar as best as I could and gave them something to eat, but I knew their lives were in danger, so I hid them on the roof. You know, with this profession, one is always prepared for the unexpected. A jealous wife had come to my bar more than once, so I was always ready for such surprises. I was always prepared to hide and lie at any moment. Sometimes, I had lost clients because of this; I always aimed to make my clientele feel safe in my bar.

I hid them and placed a cousin at the door to alert me when the king's guards arrived, as I was sure they would come. About 40 minutes later, I heard a noise. I went out dressed decently; it was the king's escort. They searched everywhere, leaving no corner unchecked, meaning on the lower part, as they were hidden above everyone's heads. Thankfully, the spies didn't sneeze, move, or, worse yet, fall on anyone's heads.

I was nervous, but I had been through this before and knew how to handle situations like these. The guards believed everything I said. They had no reason to doubt. After all, weren't we all in the same situation? Wouldn't we all be dead in the same way? In any case, I would be among the most harmed. What conquering king would spare a worn-out, mistreated, unattractive prostitute? They believed the story and went off in search with their dogs.

They came down from the roof, and I knew this was my only chance. I asked for their help and told them I believed in the power of their God. In other words, I asked them to accept me into their group and helped them escape. I wasn't sure they would help me, but it was my only hope. I had helped them, and for some strange reason, I was confident they would respond to what I had done for them.

I asked them to swear by their God, as I knew a bit about their laws from the friend I mentioned. They told me that if I truly didn't betray them, my request would be granted. I lowered them down from the wall with the same rope I had used to secretly lower many men before. But this time, the rope was an act of mercy for them and salvation for me.

They told me that when the time came for the war or the taking of the city, I should tie the same cord to a window. This cord would be the sign that I was the woman who had helped them. From that moment on, I tied the cord to my window. You don't know what happened with that cord. People kept asking why I had this cord hanging from the window, and I didn't answer.

Since that day, there was no more work at the bar; I didn't attend to any more clients. I talked to my family, brought them to my house, packed a few things, and settled them with my parents. The next day, I went out and bought enough food and prepared for the wait. People looked at me and thought I was crazy. Since I had been so worried days before, they thought I couldn't handle the pressure. But my parents believed me, as my cousin and a sister who were with me when I helped the spies had told them what happened.

The wait was a bit long, although I thought it would only be a couple of days, but it wasn't. Imagine everyone asking why we didn't leave the house. Days passed, and one very early morning, we heard the sound of a trumpet followed by the city alarm, which was only sounded in cases of extreme emergency.

I looked out of a window and saw mothers saying goodbye to their children, and the king's guards were gathering all the men of the city for war. We were all trembling, and no one wanted to leave their homes. I was a bit worried and went out to check if the cord was still visible.

A sister told me that from that place, the cord wasn't visible well. She suggested we move it, but I said no, that the cord should stay where I had lowered the spies.

It was lunchtime when a noise was heard around the city. I knew that the Israelites had made a circuit of the city and then left. Everyone was on alert and very scared.

Some speculated that perhaps Israel had regretted fighting against us, while others thought it might be a trap.

That night, I couldn't sleep, although I think no one in the city could sleep that night. We were all scared, thinking that at any moment the Hebrews would enter the city. I didn't know what to do, but one thing I did know was that I would stay inside my house no matter what.

Around 6 a.m. the next day, the alarm sounded again, and we all woke up. The Israelites were circling the walls again and then left. This time, people were even more nervous, shouting, as some thought this might be a ceremony they were performing.

Fear had fallen upon the city. To be honest, I was also scared and full of doubts, with many questions. Would those men remember me? Would they want to help a woman like me, given that they were a holy people and I was just a prostitute, a woman of ill repute?

I recalled all the stories about that holy people. I had heard that they stoned women like me, and I thought they might not want anything to do with a prostitute. But in my anguish, I remembered that they had sworn an oath, and I knew they could not break their promise.

Those six days were a nightmare. I couldn't sleep, I didn't eat, and to tell the truth, I didn't understand what was happening. It was so hot during the day, but we couldn't go out, both because of the spies' instructions and the king's orders.

On the seventh day, we were all exhausted and didn't wake up to the alarm, but when we did wake up, there was still noise. It was 3 p.m., and the Israelites were still circling the city walls. I didn't know how they didn't get tired.

Suddenly, we heard the same noise we had heard for six days, but this time it was accompanied by trumpets, horns, all sorts of instruments, and a chant in their language. The sound was mixed with other noises and felt like an earthquake.

I went to look out the window where the cord was hanging, remember? It was cloudy, and suddenly Hebrew soldiers began to enter from all sides. It was terrible. I was so scared; there were so many screams. I was on the verge of insanity until a very tall young man whom I didn't know entered my house, followed by a group of soldiers. He asked in a high voice, "Is this where Rahab lives?" I immediately answered yes, that it was me. The young man looked at me for a moment and said, "Ma'am, we have orders to protect you and your family. Follow those men, and they will take you out of this city to our camp."

At that moment, we all shouted with joy, and some of us, like me, were also crying. I had never done anything for my family; I was the black sheep. Even my siblings didn't believe what I had told them was true.

There was the prostitute being escorted out of the city like a princess. As we left the city, I cannot describe the pain in my heart seeing the land that had seen my birth being destroyed. All that beauty ruined. I glimpsed the river where I had bathed many times.

Despite the pain and with tears in my eyes, I knew I had to leave and leave everything behind. It was at that moment that I remembered I had forgotten something—I had forgotten the cord, and I knew I couldn't leave it behind. I ran to retrieve it, and a soldier followed me. I took it in my hands to keep it so I could tell this story to my grandchildren. This cord would forever remind me of how I had been saved by faith and of my former profession.

As I was leaving, everyone looked at me, but I knew I was doing the right thing. I put the cord around my neck and kept walking. Those scenes I will never forget; they were horrific—so many screams and people dying on the ground, so much blood.

I saw some of my friends dying while trying to help their children, but I couldn't do anything; I had to leave. My escape was crucial for the salvation and survival of my family and me, and I couldn't help anyone who wasn't inside my house.

I saw some friends trying to escape, and the soldiers escorting me killed them with their swords, their swords stained with blood, and their clothes torn and splattered with blood. Yet, they were kind to us, as if they knew what I had done for their comrades.

I walked away from my town, my profession, my sin, and my god, knowing that something new was coming and that I would live among a holy people, which meant I had to be holy too. I knew my life had to change, though I didn't know how—I won't lie to you—but inside me, I wanted to change.

Reflection

What a stark contrast between Rahab and Lot's wife. One fled because angels urged her, but her heart wasn't ready to leave Sodom; she stayed behind. Even though she had a God-fearing husband, she did not share his faith and didn't want to leave her homeland and people.

The other, although she had not yet left and was still in Jericho, was no longer part of the people who would be destroyed by God's instructions. One was saved by faith, and her name appears in the genealogy of Jesus Christ. She was saved because she dared to believe she could find mercy in the people she knew would defeat her nation.

The other's name is unknown; she merely became a pillar of salt.

Rahab clearly understood that she had no escape and that if she wanted to be saved, she had to leave her city and her people. She made a sound judgment of the situation and made the right decision despite her emotions.

There is a significant contrast between these two women, and although God's mercy reached both, we see from reading their stories that one was very different from the other. Just as the painting captured my attention and although there were many mountains, only one drew my eyes, so Rahab caught God's attention.

God looked at her heart and her desire to be freed from the nation that would be destroyed. And even though she was a woman not worthy of God's favor in human eyes, we see that she not only saved herself but also everyone in her house.

Some people manage to capture God's attention. Rahab is a clear example that our God is willing to change our future, which was surely eternal death, into a beautiful eternal ending with Him. Don't you think, with such a beautiful ending waiting for us with Him, that we should at least try to change our lives?

I think it's worth trying to capture God's attention, as it won't cost us much since it's precisely what He is waiting for us to do. God doesn't want us to go astray or have tragic endings like Lot's wife. He is interested in changing the hue of the picture of your life.

You are the one who has to give Him the opportunity to do something beautiful with you, just as He did with Rahab, who didn't have a lifestyle worthy of catching the attention of someone as holy and pure as our God. Rahab risked changing her life, and as a reward, she is in the story of the holy and chosen people of Israel, and also in the genealogy of our Savior, Jesus Christ.

I invite you to capture God's attention, as it won't cost you much.

CHAPTER 10

The story you are about to read is one of those stories that, even if we don't want to cry, will always bring a tear or two.

When a loved one is lost.

Mario has not been feeling well lately. He doesn't know what's wrong, but for the past couple of months, Mario has been feeling weak.

Yesterday, his wife Susana took him to the doctor, accompanied by their son Manuel.

The doctor didn't want to discuss the results of the tests with Mario, so Susana asked her son to do it while she took care of his father.

Manuel, a 20-year-old young man, is very mature for his age.

The doctor, speaking to Manuel, was somewhat pessimistic and gave no hope for Mario's survival, as his heart was very weak and the doctor thought Mario should avoid any exertion.

Susana and Manuel spoke with Mario, asking him to stop working and to take care of himself, with Manuel promising to work for him.

Six months have passed since Mario fell ill, but today he is worse. He struggles to breathe, and his pulse is barely detectable. Susana decided to go to the doctor, but before she could arrive, Mario passed away, and nothing could be done.

Only a few hours have passed since Mario's death, and Susana thought it was a dream. She regained consciousness, as she had fainted more than once, not only because of her husband's death but also because Susana is not a strong woman. In recent days, she had not eaten well while caring for Mario.

Susana, 65 years old, felt weak. She had poor eyesight and bone problems, though she was relatively well according to her recent medical reports.

Six years have now passed since Mario's death, and Susana has managed to cope with it thanks to her son Manuel.

It's a Monday at 7:20 a.m., and Susana is in the kitchen waiting for her son. She has spoken to him about finding a woman who loves him and marrying her. Susana thinks she might die at any moment, leaving her son without family. She believes her death is imminent and suggests that Manuel find a wife and have children, not only because she is 71 but also because she has lost all hope for her health since her husband died.

After about three months, Manuel found a wife, a beautiful young woman named Rebeca. He brought her to live with his mother, as she was his only remaining family.

Manuel and Rebeca had two beautiful children, who brought new joy to Susana and became her reason for living.

One morning, around 11 a.m., some of Manuel's coworkers came to inform Susana that Manuel had died. They tried to explain what had happened, but they didn't know much, as there wasn't much to tell. They said he felt a severe pain in his chest, then clutched his head, and died without speaking. Nobody knew for sure, but everyone believed it was his heart.

Manuel had been feeling unwell for about a month, experiencing headaches, dizziness, and severe chest pain. He didn't want to say anything to avoid alarming his wife and mother.

At this moment, Susana is 73 years old, almost blind, and weak. In addition, she is now a widow and has lost her only son, leaving her to console her daughter-in-law, Rebeca.

Susana is completely devastated and doesn't know what to do with her grief.

Years ago, she had lost her husband, and now she was facing the same pain, but this time it was her son—the one who had supported her for the past 8 years.

Her friends have tried to comfort her, but no one has succeeded.

Her crying is indescribable.

A friend has told her she needs to get ready for the funeral.

Now she is in front of the mirror, putting on the same clothes she wore eight years ago for her husband's funeral.

What pain! What a sad scene!

Everyone present could not contain their tears; this was so unfair and incomprehensible. Who could understand this picture of pain? Who could provide answers to this aching, powerless heart? Do you have answers?

Susana had lost the only one who looked after her, her only family. Although she thought of her two grandchildren, it did not bring her joy, as she did not know what would happen to them and their mother now.

Susana wondered: How would she explain to her grandchildren that their father would no longer be with them? They were so young that they might not even understand.

Her mind was filled with various thoughts. She worried that Rebeca might remarry and move away with her two grandchildren, leaving Susana alone and abandoned.

Susana envisioned a series of events that usually accompany the absence of a loved one.

She began walking the same path she had walked to bury her husband and say her final goodbye, but this time it was a farewell to her son and to her own life.

She walked with her head down, her face covered, her clothes torn, and ashes sprinkled on her. She was troubled and deeply sad.

From so much crying, her tears had dried, but her face reflected a woman who no longer had a reason to live.

Susana approached her son's coffin and began to fall upon the face of her deceased son.

Tears started to fall, and she thought it should be her in his place. She thought life was unfair and that God had abandoned her, believing it would have been wiser and more just for her to be the one who died instead of her only son.

As Susana was in her agony and the crowd of neighbors accompanied her, the procession stopped. She raised her face, thinking they had arrived, but realized they had not, and wondered why they had stopped.

A man she did not know approached and said, "Don't cry anymore, woman."

This statement shocked everyone, and more than one person approached and said, "Don't you see that the coffin contains her only son? How can you expect her not to cry?"

The man took her hand and wiped her tears.

By this time, everyone was murmuring, but Jesus told her not to fear. Without asking anyone's permission, He approached the deceased, looked at him intently, and said, "Young man, I say to you, arise." At that moment, there was a movement, and Manuel rose from his deathbed. Those who were carrying the dead could not believe it, and the mother herself was astonished.

Manuel looked at his mother and wife, kissed them, and everyone cried. Their tears were uncontrollable, and there were cries of joy. All present said they would not go to their homes, but Susana did not want anyone to leave. She invited everyone to celebrate, as after the funeral everyone had been with her in her sorrow, now she wanted them to join her in celebrating the joy of her son's resurrection.

Reflection:

Just like Susana, there are millions of people who lose their loved ones and do not understand why God allows it.

Talking about this fills me with sadness and compassion for those going through this kind of pain; I can barely write, tears running down my face. Oh, why do people lose their loved ones? I don't have the answers you need to hear, but I believe the only one who can meet your pain is God.

The Bible gives us many examples where Jesus encountered someone's pain, and the most beautiful thing is that He always had a solution for the problem. I don't have it, but I am sure that my God can help you understand all the questions you don't understand now.

The most important part of this story is that Jesus arrived in time. This encourages us to believe that He is interested in our pain and that He will not leave us alone on this path, one of the most difficult in life—not for the one who is leaving, but for the one who remains on earth, who has not yet earned their crown and is still flesh.

I know it is not healthy to be told not to cry, to accept God's will, and everything else that is said when someone dies. This speech is not wrong; it's just that sometimes the speaker has not put themselves in the place of the one who has suffered the loss.

I know God is a merciful God, and in His time, He will help us understand things we do not understand now.

The one who has not died does not understand many things. The one who has left, if they served God, is already in their holy place. But the person who remains must go through a process of mourning and adjustment. They have to learn to live without that person and, in many cases, face changes that can be abrupt.

What I can tell you is that God will take care of you, if you truly believe it.

Do not fear; everything will be fine, even without the person who is no longer there. Everything will work out.

He will not leave you alone.

If you want to cry, cry as much as you want, but do so with a wonderful hope that you will receive comfort.

The word says it, and I believe it: what now seems impossible to bear will tomorrow be your strongest point.

There are some things that might help you.

Do not hold back your pain; instead, let it out in a healthy way. Tell God what you think about death.

Tell Him your thoughts about what has happened; He will know how to heal you. Ask Him everything you do not understand.

Write if you can.

Listen to worship and praise music.

Find a good friend, someone who understands you and with whom you don't have to suppress your feelings.

Seek God in times of meditation and ask Him to speak to your life.

Do not listen to all the comments and assumptions people make about what has happened.

If necessary, seek help from people who can guide you on what to do now.

If you have children, do not lie to them. Tell them the truth and pray for them. I always told my children that death is an absolutely natural thing, that they should not fear it or feel sad about talking about it. It's true that we will miss the people who have left us and that we cry, but not because the person is now in a bad place, but because we won't see them for the moment.

That is: "for the moment, you won't see them again," but if you are firm in God, one day you will meet them in heaven.

I don't know about you, but I have a few people I am eager to see again. To be honest, I miss them terribly. They are on my mind and in my heart now and always will be, as I loved them beyond my strength.

Here is my list of loved ones who are no longer with me: my grandmother, my grandfather, my brother, my mother, and a couple of wonderful friends. I miss them, I cannot lie, but I have a wonderful hope that I will see them very soon, whether Christ comes or I go. But one thing I am sure of is that I have not lost them forever; it is only "for a moment."

I will see them. This is my hope and yours too!

CHAPTER 11

Sofía's Story

Sofía is my next character, and she had to face rejection—not just from one person, but from many. She was ill, and this was difficult to endure in the place where she lived.

The Rejection

I never knew Sofía personally, but someone who did—her best friend—not only knew her story but lived through this sad experience with her. She shared the story with me, and I found it fascinating, so I want to share it with you.

Josefa was Sofía's friend and had been a witness to 18 years of pain and anguish.

Josefa told me that Sofía had already passed away, and one day she received a message from one of Sofía's sons, who wanted to see her. This didn't seem strange to Josefa, so she immediately went to her late friend's house.

After being there for about 15 minutes, Sofía's eldest son, along with his father and Sofía's other two children, brought out a package that read: "With love for my only friend, Josefa."

Sofía's husband was present and signaled to his children to take Josefa upstairs, where there were also several packages. It was Sofía's clothing and jewelry—this had been her final wish. Sofía had no daughters, nor any female relatives, so she decided that Josefa should have all that was hers.

When Josefa returned home, she didn't feel like opening those packages—she wasn't ready.

Two months passed, and one day she felt she had the strength to open the package. Inside was a small letter of gratitude from her friend, but what really caught Josefa's attention was a diary in which Sofía had written about all her suffering during those 18 years.

The letters were a bit smudged, as if water had fallen on them. You could somewhat understand what was written and sense the suffering Sofía had experienced when she wrote the diary.

After Josefa talked with me, we decided to read the diary, not just to learn what Sofía had gone through, but also to help other women who might be in a similar situation.

Here are some excerpts from Sofía's diary:

January 12
"Today, I feel very bad. I don't know what's wrong with me. Although I am a young woman, I feel like an old lady. I think I will have to see the doctor. I have a sharp pain in my back that almost keeps me from straightening up."

January 26
"Every day is worse. Today, I can hardly walk; when I do, the pain is unbearable, even breathing causes pain. Today, I will get the results of my tests. I hope it's nothing serious because I don't want to die and leave my young children without a mother."

January 27
"Yesterday, I went to the doctor. He said I won't get better. He told me he doesn't know what's wrong with me, that he can only help me manage the pain and that I must learn to live with this illness."

April 13
"It has been three months since the doctor told me he couldn't help me. I've lost my feminine charm; I look like

a 50-year-old woman when I'm really 30. I don't know what to do; even my clothes don't fit with this hump growing on my back. I have no friends except Josefa, and my husband no longer wants to go out with me because he's embarrassed by me."

October 2

"It's been a couple of years since I last wrote. Today, I decided to write again because writing makes me feel like someone is listening. I've been praying in church, and I feel that somehow God has heard my prayers since I'm still alive and watching my three children grow. I hardly go out, only to Josefa's house and the temple to pray. Who knows, maybe one day God will remember me."

The following excerpt was written when she had been suffering from her illness for 15 years:

July 24

"My children have grown up. I've completed my task. My husband has another woman because I can't even have relations anymore. He is a good man, but it's not fair for him to be condemned to a woman who looks like an animal, or worse, a monster. I don't want to go to church anymore; I feel like I'm the center of attention. Everyone looks at me as if I were something strange and they reject me. I've stopped asking God to live. I think it might even be better for my children if I die."

Three years later...

December 8

"Every day, I can move less. I don't want to live anymore. I've been waiting for a miracle for 18 years, but it might never come. Maybe this is God's punishment, but now that I've lost my youth, I don't want to continue living in this shame. When I go to the temple, I don't feel loved; people look at me as if I were unclean, even the priest avoids me and doesn't greet me. Who would want to notice a woman who is not only old but also deformed? I've endured all these years patiently out of love for my children, but I'm tired now, and I want to die in peace."

These were the last words we found in her diary.

But the story didn't end here. The following week, Josefa invited her friend to the temple, picked her up, and they went together to worship God.

On Saturdays, special services were held at the temple, but Sofía no longer had the strength to worship. As she entered the temple, she went to a separate place and began to cry, which was not uncommon for her. But this time, she felt something inside her that had been preventing her from worshipping was breaking.

That Saturday was special; there was something different in the place. She lifted her eyes and realized there was a new preacher. He was different and genuinely cared about people. When he saw her, he called her over and said, "Woman, you are free from your illness," and then placed his hands on her hump. This was very unusual, as no one ever touched her, especially not a man, let alone a preacher.

She doesn't know what happened, but immediately she felt like someone was lifting the burden she had carried for 18 years. She couldn't believe it, and neither could Josefa, her friend, who shared this story with me.

The two of them began to praise God so loudly that everyone in the temple noticed what was happening. Josefa didn't know much of what happened afterward because her friend was crying so much that she decided to take her outside and bring her home.

From that day on, Sofía seemed like a different woman, even appearing younger. She regained her self-esteem, and the people who had once rejected her now wanted to be her friends. She reconciled with her husband and lived 30 more years after that, passing away naturally of old age.

PART THREE:

THE WOMAN, HER DESIRES

&

HER GOALS

CHAPTER 12

The Difficulty of the Search

It's the year 2005. It's 11 o'clock in the morning, and I'm on a train heading to a place called Venray. Venray is a small town in the Netherlands located near Germany. I'm going to visit a friend who recently lost her husband.

During this journey, I've been feeling strange sensations, maybe because I'm traveling alone, as I usually travel with my husband. Another reason could be that I'm unfamiliar with the place I'm going to.

Whenever I travel, it's always an experience for me, whether good or not so good, and this one I would categorize as one of those I call regular.

I don't know the place I'm going, which makes me very alert to every movement around me.

At this moment, we're arriving at one of my stops. It's the station of a small town, and because of this, I believe it has few amenities, not like the station in the city where I live, which is a station with everything a traveler needs.

Let me describe how I feel. I feel that I don't have enough information to reach the place where I need to go, although one thing I'm sure of is that I will get where I need to go.

Now my journey has ended. It's been three days since I wrote what you just read. Today is Sunday, and I'm in a small station, waiting for my train. I've just heard that my train is delayed by 10 minutes. This is not a problem for the passengers who are waiting, except for me, I think, because this delay means I will miss my next train.

Now I'm at another station; I've missed my train and have to wait an hour for the next one. I've waited the hour, not very patiently, but I've waited. Now I'm on the train that will take me home.

There are situations like this, being on a train heading home, knowing the place I'm going to, but not knowing the place where I am. It's a bit difficult because you have to find the transport that will take you to your final destination. You have to find the correct exits to make the connections and then make sure you're on the right train.

At this moment, the train conductors have checked my ticket, and I feel a bit better because I know I'm on the right train.

When I was coming back to this place, I had different sensations or emotions from those I have now. I didn't know where I was going, nor did I know the stations where I had to stop to catch another train. And worst of all, in the country I'm in, they don't speak my language. So, when I don't know something, or I'm not sure, I ask how I can do it.

The outbound train to my friend's not only had a delay, but, to top it off, it also changed its departure gate. They announced it, I heard the announcement a bit late and only understood that it was about my train and a change, but I didn't know which change, since I'm still not used to this language.

Then, as I saw people moving downstairs, I assumed I had to ask someone. The man I asked couldn't tell me; he only knew what I knew—that the train in front of us wasn't going where I was going. I knew that too because, luckily, I can read this language.

At this moment, I knew I didn't have much time, so I decided to follow the crowd without asking. We were all in a hurry, and no one would have had time to answer me if I had asked something.

Even though I was following the crowd, I didn't feel at peace because the thought that this crowd might be heading towards another destination, different from mine, kept crossing my mind.

When I was halfway there, I heard the announcement again, and this time I paid full attention and could understand the announcement and the changes.

I kept following the crowd because I don't know this station, but I knew where I was heading because I read the signs, which guided me to my exit—the same one the crowd I was following was seeking.

When I arrived, the train was already full, waiting for the passengers who were slow. I was one of them because, although I wanted to hurry, it's not as easy for me as it is for Europeans, who have long legs, and one of their steps is like three of mine.

Luckily, apart from the change in the departure gate, the train was also delayed, perhaps due to the same change, to give slow people like me time.

Once inside the train, I settled in, but while waiting for the departure time, I made sure I was on the right train by asking. Incidentally, the young woman I asked was also going to one of my stops, although she wasn't sure if she was on the right train either. She knew the route but was a bit confused because of the change.

A few minutes after sitting down, a couple of hurried old ladies arrived, also asking. Although they knew the language, they weren't sure if this was their train due to the change. After they had settled in, a man who overheard them speaking told them that this train wouldn't pass by where they were going, so they had to get off in a hurry.

All these things made me think about life itself and our destination, where we are going, and the paths we take to get there. I started to think that life is very similar to this journey. Often, we get on the wrong train, and sometimes we're on the right train, but we get off at the wrong stop.

How do we know in our lives that we are doing the right thing? How do we know that we are heading where God wants us to go? How do we know if we should change, and when, how, where, or maybe with whom?

In this life, some situations are more difficult than going to a place we've never been. Anyway, this journey of life is one we only live once. There is no reincarnation; we are in this life to live once, and this is something many have misinterpreted, as if trying to justify their sin. But I believe there's a way to walk this life, and that guide is God.

If we want to know if we are doing the right thing, the Bible will guide us, the life of Jesus even more. God has given us the Holy Spirit to guide us in case we need advice. Is He your guide? If you don't know, you can ask God. I believe in the guiding hand of God. I believe that if we ask Him, He will not give us the wrong direction.

It's true that due to changes in schedules or exits, we may be a little confused, but this is no excuse to take any train. Anyway, it's up to you to be interested in reaching your destination.

Life is like a journey.

At a train station, there are different trains, but there are also different passengers with different destinations. Although we are all in the same station, not everyone has the same goal; not everyone is going to the same destination.

We may even take the same train, but not everyone will get off at the same stop. Some go first, and others later. What is certain is that we are all traveling because we want to reach a place.

Where do you want to go? Do you want to meet God? How do you think you will meet Him if you don't seek Him? How will you get answers if you don't ask questions? If you realize you're on the wrong train, what do you do? The logical thing is to get off the train at the next stop and ask how you can get to where you want to go.

CHAPTER 13

What Is Truth?

> "And you will know the truth,
> and the truth will set you free."
> —*Jesus*

There are many types of truths. Truth is that which can be proven, verified, or for which there is evidence. Each of us knows truths, but "the truth" refers to a specific truth. That truth is Jesus—what an elegant term for our Lord.

Jesus was genuine, real, and true. In Him, there were no lies, no facades, nor did He reflect anything that He was not. He was exactly as He appeared.

Could we say the same about ourselves?

This week (2006), I watched a television show that my daughter Abigail really enjoys. This show is about a teenager who has magical powers. This young girl with strange powers decided to bake a chocolate cake, but not just any cake—this was a special cake because instead of baking powder, she added a special powder that had the power to make people tell the truth, even if they didn't want to.

Anyone who ate this delicious cake would immediately say everything they were thinking, not what they wanted to say or what the other person wanted to hear.

It took just 24 hours to throw an entire high school into complete chaos.

One of my favorite scenes was of the principal, announcing over the school's PA system what he did every Friday and with whom—something that was a secret, of course, because of his reputation in front of the students.

Another amusing situation involved three inseparable friends who, on that day, told each other everything they truly thought. That ended their "friendship" immediately. Why? Because that relationship wasn't real; it was based on lies and, above all, hypocrisy.

Sometimes we want to be surrounded by sincerity and truth. This is especially true for women, as this is one of the needs women have. We women like sincerity. But why do you lie, why are you hypocritical? Why do you accept lies and hypocrisy as part of your life?

It's because women are afraid—yes, they are afraid of being rejected for who they are, so they prefer to live in a world of lies and feed on mutual hypocrisy.

I can imagine what this world would be like if we all ate that cake that makes you tell the truth.

All women would be exposed for their true age, size, and weight. Their secret relationships and their lies about their "friends" would be revealed.

If we want sincerity, we must be sincere ourselves, and if we don't like hypocrisy, then we shouldn't be hypocrites ourselves.

God's desire is for His children to come to know Him so that we may find true freedom. Yes, because it's not freedom when we have to appear to be something we're not, when we have to pretend to feel what we don't, just to be accepted by others.

God will accept us without masks. He wants you to be yourself, to be what you say you are, to be on the inside what you seem to be on the outside.

The Bible contains many verses that tell us that what is hidden will one day be brought to light.

If we have come to know Jesus, if we have eaten from that spiritual cake that has the power to make us stop being hypocrites, then we will know freedom.

Many will reject you because you will be different, but it doesn't matter, because in this way you will please God.

CHAPTER 14

Loosen the Bonds from Your Neck

It was a winter night in 2002. Normally, during the winter, I feel a bit tired and sleepy early, but this night, though I was tired, I didn't feel sleepy. This was one of those nights when God draws me to be with Him.

It was almost two in the morning, and after making sure that I was talking to myself, since my husband had fallen asleep without me noticing, and now hearing his snores, I knew he wouldn't finish the evening with me.

I got up and went to the kitchen to make some tea, preparing myself to hear what my Father wanted to tell me.

After preparing the tea, I went to the living room. For a moment, I looked out the window and saw how everything was covered in snow. I thought, "It looks so beautiful from here, but being outside might not be as pleasant, as the cold from the snow sometimes prevents us from enjoying how beautiful it is."

I knelt in front of the heater, but I couldn't stay in that position for long because I was tired. However, for an obvious reason to me, I knew I had better stay awake, because if I went to bed, I wouldn't sleep, and neither would my husband. When I can't sleep, I toss and turn so much that inevitably the person next to me ends up waking up too.

So I sat down. I had finished my cup of tea and was meditating on God when I started to fall asleep and dream a strange dream. This was my dream:

I was in a place that seemed like a cemetery, or maybe it was. There were many women of all sizes and nationalities—tall and short. Blonde women, brunettes, olive-skinned, redheads, women from the Middle East, Asians, and Africans. There were all kinds of women, but there was something that made them all the same: their clothing. Yes, they all wore the same kind of clothes, if you could even call those rags clothes. But aside from being rags, they were torn and old.

Another thing they all had in common was that they were dragging chains on their feet; some were tied together with the same chains. They also had some kind of rope around their necks, which hung like a decorative necklace, but it was a kind of rotten rope.

The dresses of these women were all the same—gray and colorless. These dresses had no specific style. The appearance of these women was strange; they seemed lifeless, acting like robots. Their faces didn't express sadness or pain—they expressed nothing. Although I could see that they were beautiful women, there was a shade over them that prevented them from appearing as they truly were.

They had ashes on their bodies and walked aimlessly, without wanting to reach any place, moving in circles. They also emitted screams—screams that would scare anyone.

I was watching all of this, which left me perplexed when I realized that I was among them, in the same place, though a little apart, and they were unaware of my presence.

For some strange reason, I began to feel uncomfortable—truthfully, I was angry. I asked myself why I was there, how I had come to this place. I wasn't one of them, and to be honest, I didn't understand anything.

I was thinking and decided to complain to an office, though I don't know how I knew of its existence. I said to myself, "I'll go talk to Gabriel, I'll complain, and they'll have to get me out of here."

One of the things that made me not want to be there was the rotten smell that I could barely stand.

I decided to go talk to the Archangel Gabriel—yes, you read that right.

I walked toward a path that reflected a lot of light. This path was located in front of the place where these women lived, but it seemed that the light bothered them, perhaps because the place they lived in was a bit dark.

I began to walk this path. It was a strange and small path, but somewhat long, leading to the office where I intended to file my complaint. When I arrived, it was a glass house surrounded by a lot of light, as bright as the lights in stadiums.

I arrived and told a young person—I'm not sure of the sex, as they were wearing only a white robe and had long hair but no discernible gender. This creature was managing some books, though I don't know what they were.

When they saw me, they attended to me immediately with great kindness and asked what I needed. I told them I needed to speak with Gabriel. They said this wasn't possible, as Gabriel wasn't there to attend to any women. Apparently, he had a specific function, though I didn't know what it was.

I was so angry that I didn't want to hear what they were saying and kept complaining and calling out for Gabriel.

The person told me they could help me and asked what was wrong. I said, "I don't understand why I'm here in this horrible place. It smells bad, and it's dark. Besides, those women frighten me, they make me feel afraid, and I don't want to be here. You're mistaken, this is not the place for me, I want to get out of here." By this point, I was shouting and crying.

I made such a fuss that the person had to go and get Gabriel. I kept quiet while listening to what they were saying to Gabriel, though from a distance.

The person said, "Gabriel, this woman is breaking the rules, I don't know how she got in here. This woman is strange; she doesn't want to be in that place. The other women never complain; in fact, when we try to help them leave, they almost always refuse. If it weren't for the Holy Spirit working with them, we'd never be able to get them out. This woman says she's here by mistake—what should I do?"

Gabriel replied, laughing, "Can't you see the brightness in her eyes, that her clothes are different, and that she's aware of everything? Look at her—she's alive."

The person said, "What?"

Gabriel replied, "Yes, she has life in her—the life of our God. That's why you won't be able to silence her, because she can see clearly what the others cannot."

The person asked, "Then what should I do with her?"

Gabriel replied, "Nothing."

I was expecting him to say, "Take her out of here since she's different," but no, he said to do nothing.

When he said this, I approached with tears in my eyes. He looked at me tenderly and said, "I know you're alive, but you have to be here."

At that moment, I woke up.

When I woke up, it was 4 in the morning. My neck hurt, and I felt a bit strange because I hadn't understood the revelation. When I got up to go to bed, the Spirit of God came upon me and said, "Don't go to sleep; write down the vision," and so I did.

When I finished, I went to the kitchen and made another cup of tea. After drinking it, I went to bed. By this time, it was 5 in the morning.

For almost a year, I didn't understand the meaning of this vision, although one thing comforted me—the words I had heard, that I was alive.

When I finally understood this vision, believe me, I cried so much that my eyes swelled because I felt deep sorrow for the condition of the woman without the life of God in her.

That vision is not so difficult to understand if we do so in the spirit.

This vision reminded me of a woman described in Isaiah 52. In this vision, Isaiah saw a woman condemned to loneliness—a loneliness where, although surrounded by others, she still feels alone. But where does this loneliness, abandonment, and sadness come from? It comes from the depths of her being, from her soul, from the essence of who she is.

In this vision, there are things that the Spirit revealed to me that I want to share with you. In the following chapters, I will describe the meanings of each symbol that God showed me in that vision.

CHAPTER 15

The Place Where the Women Lived

This place seemed like a cemetery, a place where only the dead dwell. It was not only lifeless, colorless, and without light, but it also smelled bad. This place is a spiritual realm; it represents the state in which the woman finds herself. The place she has chosen to live in is without life, without light, and will lead her to destruction.

This place is a spiritual state. The woman has allowed the world to influence her in such a way that she doesn't realize that the path she is walking leads to ruin. This condition came as a consequence of Eve being deceived by the devil and accepting his lies that they would be like God.

For this reason, a woman without God in her life cannot escape this place. But glory to God! There is hope—Christ came to destroy the works of the devil.

This place is the world itself and its way of life. Even though the woman doesn't realize that she is following a pattern that does not come from God, in essence, it will lead to her own death, speaking spiritually. The world is far from God, and this generation does not want to follow the statutes established by God in His Word.

One thing that caught my attention was that in front of this place, there was a path that reflected a lot of light. It was a place positioned there with the sole purpose of offering help to any woman in need, because God does not want anyone to perish or have any excuses.

Although this place was enveloped in darkness, the woman who lived there had the opportunity to leave if she wanted to. The main problem is that when someone is in such a situation, they cannot see. The eyes of those women seemed unable to perceive that very near them was an escape. I believe they weren't even aware of the seriousness of their situation.

When I arrived there, I realized it immediately, but my condition was different because the life of God is at work in me. I could smell the stench of that place, while they didn't seem to notice it. I saw the darkness of that place and felt uncomfortable, but they walked around as if they were at home, as if they were accustomed to it.

It is so sad to perceive the condition of this world, and how it is without God.

This place is a spiritual realm, meaning that not only are those who are not Christians there, but anyone in one of these situations could unknowingly be bound or chained.

CHAPTER 16

The Clothes the Women Wore

These clothes, or as I would call them, "tattered rags," represent the attitudes of each woman in the world. It doesn't matter where she's from; all women are vulnerable and sensitive to emotional damage in this sense. All women have the same emotional needs, although some express them more than others.

This is something our enemy knows, and for this reason, he begins to emotionally damage women from the moment they are born. He knows that if he can damage a woman, he will have a future filled with victories, whether in the family or outside of it.

Every woman has been wounded, hurt, mistreated, and even if she tries to appear otherwise, deep down she is damaged. These clothes are the garments that the world wants women to wear—clothes of pain, bitterness, depression. In other words, clothes that reflect death, that smell bad, and that are torn, which are not the clothes that belong to a child of God, an heir of His grace.

God wants your inner self to be dressed in the garments of the Spirit that He has prepared for you. He wants to clothe you in the attire of a princess and give you a ring. He wants to crown you and make you feel important. He wants to crown you with joy and gladness and have you dwell with Him in heavenly places.

But the world and the circumstances of life have made you dress incorrectly. The world is a liar and wants to make you its ally so that with your actions and attitude, you contribute to the growth of its kingdom.

These clothes represent many things. They are the armor you have created to protect yourself from being hurt again, but that armor will not prevent harm. What it does is delay your liberation from that place and your escape. It prevents you from being able to perceive the works of darkness.

The world's objective is to make you insensitive and hard, which is not characteristic of women, as God created women to be sensitive and capable of love and forgiveness. The enemy's goal is to make you dwell in places of darkness, which symbolically represent death, so that the life within you cannot emerge.

CHAPTER 17

Chains Dragged by the Feet

These chains represent habits and customs that you've adopted as part of your personality but that, in reality, have prevented you from truly living and enjoying life naturally. These are things you've come to accept as normal, but they are actually the influence of the world's system, directed by the prince of this world.

These chains drag you along with the crowd, leading you to live in a way that, to ordinary people who aren't interested in truly living, seems natural. When I say "truly living," I mean enjoying eternal life on this earth in a natural way and the eternal life that God has prepared for you in the future.

These chains are ministering spirits whose goal is to destroy you, kill you, ruin you, and steal everything that God has given you. These spirits enter your life as a result of sins committed without regard for God's Word. In this way, the enemy gradually binds you and drags you closer to his plans—to destroy you and prevent you from becoming a woman of God. He knows that if you manage to escape this state, if you remove those garments and dress in the correct ones, and if you close the doors to sin, the chains will break.

The chains on the feet signify that he wants to bind you so that you cannot live in the freedom of the gospel and the holiness that God desires for His children. The feet symbolize the place where you should put on the shoes of the gospel, but if they are symbolically bound, how can a woman with chains on her feet wear the shoes of the gospel?

These chains, dragged by these women, are nothing more than the things that keep a woman from seeking God. There are different types of bindings, depending on each person. There are bad influences (people who lead you to do wrong). There are places that aren't good for your spiritual life. There are practices that seem normal but end up harming you. What begins as a simple youthful game can ultimately separate you from God for eternity.

Sometimes we ignore the small things we do, not realizing that those small things will eventually create a chasm between us and God. In the vision God gave me, I saw some women bound together by chains—not all, but some were united by them. This means that there are women who are a bad influence on others, and not only do they fall, but they also drag others down with them, whether consciously or unconsciously.

There are women who are a bad influence, even if they are our friends or family. Whether it's a sister, an aunt, or even a mother, if you feel that she is not on the right path, this means that God has opened your eyes to see. So, don't let yourself be dragged down.

We must learn to separate friendships from what is vital to our spiritual, emotional, and even economic life. After all, it is very dangerous to follow the path of others. It's important to ensure that your friends share the same perspective as you, that they think like you. The Word says, "How can two walk together unless they are agreed?" You should always seek out people who are closer to God than you are. The Word also says, "Can the blind lead the blind? Will they not both fall into a pit?" Your goal is not to fall into the same situation as another woman, is it? I believe no one wants to end up badly.

CHAPTER 18

The Necklace Around the Neck

These symbolize bonds and represent sins related to sexual immorality. They distort how women perceive sex, turning it into the opposite of what God intended from the beginning. The world has created a sexual system that degrades women to their lowest level as human beings.

It's important to recognize that this condition in the world we live in is alarming, especially for women. Though for this generation, it's considered entirely normal.

Why women? Because they believe that since they are physically attractive, they should take advantage of it, and Satan knows this path will lead them away from their true essence. This happens when he gets women to focus more on the physical than the spiritual, when he succeeds in making women expose their bodies, which should be holy, to prostitution, fornication, and adultery.

Even though women have fallen into this degrading condition, deep down, they don't really want to live like this. If we talk to a woman in such a degrading situation, and if she's honest with us, we'll realize that she wouldn't choose to be in that condition if she had a choice.

This condition is not directly imposed by the devil, as God showed me that the women didn't have chains around their necks but rather a type of rope with a couple of knots, like a makeshift necklace, but it was partially rotten. This symbolizes the carnal desires of women; the fact that it was rotten means that women can remove them from their necks simply by pulling them off. This condition in women arises from their unwillingness to give God the place He deserves.

God created women with the intention that they be loved, but Satan has trapped them in the snares of uncontrolled sex. He has made them live for their desires, convincing them that life is about gratifying the flesh. Women don't realize that by doing this, they are only inviting more emotional pain into their lives and, in many cases, an untimely death.

Women must come to understand that they need to con-
secrate their bodies by removing these ropes from their
necks—ropes that should be a source of shame but are
now publicly displayed as if they were an adornment,
where everyone knows what we do. Today, these sins
have become so normalized that they seem to decorate
the lives of those who bear them.

These ropes are not only worn by women who practice
prostitution but also by all those who engage in sex outside of marriage.

CHAPTER 19

Ashes on the Clothes

These ashes symbolize the vanity of life, and if anyone wants a synonym for vanity, they would likely choose two words: *female sex*. The world has created a system to trap women; commerce knows that women are often vain, which is why it creates products to entrap them and profit from them as consumers.

Cosmetics, clothes, shoes, and the perfume industry seem never-ending, not to mention jewelry, whether real or costume. Women are special beings; when God created them, He made them stand out from all other creatures. However, women have a need to be admired and praised, and if this need isn't guided by the Holy Spirit, it can become harmful.

In the end, women have come to believe that looking good on the outside is enough. They have created a façade of who they really are, allowing themselves to be led by the masses and fashion, which dictates how they should dress, smell, and look.

The world has created a system that is not from God and suggests to women what is "perfect." But the only thing women gain from this system is frustration, as we are even told what measurements we need to have to be considered perfect, according to what they define as perfection.

This is why God showed me ashes because they merely cloud what is real and true, making women feel less beautiful every day. It's a bit difficult to understand, but so much advertising toward consumerism has only made women feel less beautiful, leading them to believe that if they don't consume certain products, they will lose something others have.

There are products that are essential in life, and others that have become part of our routine, but we women are not plastic dolls or mannequins, for the prince of this world to suggest that we should all look the same. God created each woman with her own unique figure (separate from being overweight, which is another issue). Not every woman can have the same face, the same eyes, the same waist, the same hair color, and on top of that, wear the same clothes.

This is what fashion does to women: it turns them into dolls, stripping them of their power to make decisions. Fashion, in God's eyes, is like dust. Why? Because it's fleeting and it obscures your true beauty.

We cannot truly live without fashion, because everything in life is fashion, whether old or new. But we cannot let any fashion cause us to lose our identity as individuals. Nor can we fall into fanaticism and declare that all these things are bad—no. But it's true that if we want to be real and free, we must find a balance.

CHAPTER 20

Without a Fixed Direction

These women seemed to have no goals, as if they were just living for the sake of living. One of God's objectives is to draw us to Him, but often, we do nothing to achieve that connection. These women did not want to reach any destination. This is part of Satan's work—he does not want people to have goals in life or to strive to reach any destination.

If you want to achieve something in your life, you have to sit down and think about how you will accomplish it. If you want to go somewhere, you will have to walk to get there, because desire alone is not enough. You must want to reach a place in order to actually arrive there.

Some people say they are waiting for God to change them, but they never do anything to improve their situation. They are always waiting for some extraordinary miracle to happen, without realizing that this is not how it works. God wants to help all the women in the world, but they have to ask for it. They have to surrender their egos so that God can work in their lives.

These women who walked without a fixed direction represent how, when someone is bound by sin and by the devil, they often don't realize they are walking aimlessly—without a specific destination. This happens for two reasons:

First, because Satan does not allow you to see the end of the path you are on. He doesn't want you to realize that it's not in your best interest, because, in the end, you will be the one who suffers the most.

The second reason is that, even if you wanted to perceive spiritual things and the mysteries of this life, you wouldn't be able to do so in a carnal way. The Bible says, "The natural person does not accept the things of the Spirit of God, for they are folly to him, and he is not able to understand them because they are spiritually discerned."

CHAPTER 21

Screams that Send Shivers and Frighten

I never stopped to think about why these women were screaming. Their screams were ones of desperation, making me want to leave that place immediately. Those screams have stayed with me to this day.

God revealed to me what this signifies: the pain and desperation that those women experience in that place. The pain caused by the chains and the overwhelming darkness. The pain because, even though they are not alive, deep down they know that something better exists.

This pain is what causes many women to curse their children and always have negative words on their lips. The scream was the only sign of the internal condition of those women, as, though in the spirit, what God allowed me to see were their souls. I saw them cry and, more than that, scream like the possessed. These screams came from their souls.

This scream is a sign that the condition of the woman is not entirely lost; there is still hope that deep down she wants to change. This scream makes the woman aware of her need. Even if she cannot perceive the full extent of her bondage, she knows she needs God, and God responds to this cry of anguish.

The sign that God is interested in your pain and wants to deliver you is that His heavenly presence is near you.

CHAPTER 22

The Heavenly Outpost

The path in front of that horrible place symbolizes the mercy of heaven within your reach. God is so interested in helping you escape from that prison of darkness. He has spiritual offices ready to work on your behalf.

God has sent His angels and even an archangel, if necessary, to guard you and help you get out. You are not alone; the Almighty is on your side, and you and He are in the majority.

All you need to do is allow yourself to be touched by His mighty hand. He has not only done this, but He has also sent someone who is free to be close to you, so that together you can achieve your liberation.

Think for a moment: Has God sent someone to your side and you haven't considered it? What kind of person is it? Is this someone who wants to bring you closer to God? This person may be a messenger from God to help you with your pain.

Don't let this person pass through your life without allowing God to complete the purpose for which they were sent. Look at the fruit of the Holy Spirit in them and imitate the good things in their life. Pray to God to show you how to be guided by His servant and listen to her voice as if it were God's. If this woman lives according to God's word, then she is truly His messenger. Take advantage of her presence before she is taken from your side.

CHAPTER 23

Failure Doesn't Change You

Failure doesn't change you or make you bitter as we might think; it only reveals what we truly are.

The Labyrinths of Failure

A month ago, I watched the most important match of the 2004 Euro Cup, held in Portugal. My family and I were prepared for what we expected to be an exciting game. We had popcorn, cold soda, and a friend over. Everything was perfect, and we all gathered in front of the television.

We were all looking forward to a great game, including my oldest son, Neftalí, who is 11. After the first half, I noticed something was wrong. I couldn't understand how a strong team like Portugal could still be at 0.

I had seen a few of their games, and they had won almost always. They were so good that it was no surprise they were in the final; I was almost sure they would win the Euro Cup that year. Even though I don't know much about football, I enjoy watching matches with my husband for two reasons: to share what he likes and to ask questions about things I don't understand, though I don't always get immediate answers. He usually explains things so I can let him watch the game peacefully.

During the first 15-minute break, I told my husband what I thought, and he agreed that something was wrong. He explained that Greece, the opposing team, had previously defeated Portugal in a qualifying match. Now Portugal had to face Greece again, but this time for a greater victory.

Portugal's team was fearful of losing to Greece again. As a result, when they nearly scored a goal, they became so nervous that they couldn't accurately calculate their shots, resulting in no goals.

Throughout the match, I saw many potential goals go awry because the team wasn't focused enough to score. Greece defeated Portugal despite a fierce battle because Portugal was more focused on preventing Greece from scoring than on their own goal-scoring opportunities. Portugal was defeated not just by the opposing team but by a greater enemy: their own minds and fear.

The players were haunted by their previous failure and did not focus on the upcoming challenge. They concentrated on stopping their opponents instead of pursuing their own goals.

We all want to be winners, but many forget that failures offer valuable lessons. From failures, we learn to be stronger and to keep our eyes on what truly matters, our greater objectives.

Do you know what your goals are? Have you learned from your failures?

I have learned the following:

1. *We are not as good as we think we are.*

2. *We are not as humble as we pretend to be.*

3. *We are not as faithful as we claim to be.*

Failure reveals who we truly are. It exposes the raw material we are made of. If you are weak, proud, vain, manipulative, capricious, angry, deceitful, or critical, failure will bring these traits to light.

Failure is like a bitter taste in our mouths that doesn't go away easily; it needs time. Failure is one of the many lenses of life that makes us see things differently from how they truly are. It doesn't change us or make us bitter; it only shows us our true selves.

It removes the masks we sometimes wear in front of others. Failure can be your greatest ally for success or your worst enemy in destroying you. It won't destroy you; it will let you choose one of its tools.

When we fail, we can decide what to do next: fight and try again, or let the defeat end us. Which tool will you use? Will you choose the one that teaches you to start over or the one that tells you that you are a failure with no future?

Failure can be your greatest ally for triumph and a new beginning, this time with experience. There is nothing worse in life than failing and feeling like a failure. There is no greater victor than one who can lift their head and start anew from their failure.

CHAPTER 24

The Story of a Failure

This is the story of a father who loved his children and provided everything they needed without lacking anything. His name was Adonaí Shalom. He had raised his children with dedication and had never failed them. Adonaí was perfect. Unlike us parents, he had no issues with himself. He did not spend time healing himself; he understood his children's needs and was never apart from them. His children were part of him and shared his DNA. From a young age, he observed that they resembled him.

Adonaí felt happy, and nothing marred his joy. Occasionally, he would chuckle while watching his oldest son grow up, believing that his son would, when he grew up, be like him, think like him, and reign like him. More than once, his servants heard him speak about his children and the plans he had for them. He was one of those parents who daydreamed about the great future his descendants would have.

He prepared everything, not wanting his children to lack anything. He had no problem with money, time, or space; he could fulfill his will without interference. He had plans and decided to grant his children dominion and power just as he had. He did not want anyone to say that Adonaí was stingy. He prepared a future for them filled not only with joy and love but also with power and authority.

Adonaí was a king, and his word could change things. So, he decided to create another kingdom separate from his own, a realm where his children could feel comfortable in their own space. His children were surrounded by everything. When I say everything, I mean everything. They had a beautiful land, a paradise, especially for them to reign without issue.

Like any father, Adonaí had a few rules his children had to follow. He believed this would not be a problem. Everything was going well. He visited them every afternoon, and they were a great family—a perfect family, one might say.

Adonaí had an enemy, the only one, but he was wounded and sought revenge. When this enemy learned of the existence of Adonaí's children, he resolved to destroy them. One day, plotting how to harm Adonaí, this enemy thought of killing his children.

When he arrived at the place where the children reigned, it was a beautiful afternoon, and the sun was setting slowly, as if reluctant to leave. He stopped to observe, and his heart was filled with rage upon seeing the perfect love and communication between father and children. He felt envious not only of Adonaí but also of the children who had dominion and a kingdom to rule, something he had always dreamed of while serving Adonaí.

He thought to himself, "It won't be enough to kill them. I'll do something better. I'll make them no longer a happy family. I'll enter them and deceive them. I'll make them fail their father and thus exact my revenge. I'll take away their dominions and they won't be able to reign. I'll expel them from this place and make them my slaves. I'll exact double revenge on Adonaí and enjoy every day watching them sink into the mud as my slaves. I'll reduce them to nothing, making them see they are no kings, only I am the king."

That afternoon, the enemy did nothing but spent days observing from afar how to enter that perfect place without being discovered. For many days, he plotted. One day, while observing, he realized he had found the perfect ally, and thus, he discovered how to destroy the children of the king.

Those children fell into the trap set by the enemy, and Adonaí was devastated by the loss of his children. These children were ungrateful for believing in someone more than their father. They were unjust for failing their father, who had given them everything. Don't you think?

It is true they didn't know the enemy, and it is true they were deceived, but I wonder: Where did they find the strength to betray their father? What made them forget that everything they had was given by Adonaí? How could they forget so much dedication from their father? What were they missing when they had dominion and a kingdom?

This father did not sit down to cry over his great failure. No, he did not become bitter. Adonaí could have done so. He could have decided not to have more children, could have told one of his servants not to serve his children anymore, or even could have caused their death. He was a king, and what happened was a conspiracy against his kingdom, but he did none of this. Do you know why? Because he loved his children. The nature of this king is love and mercy. The love of this king was greater than the circumstances.

Not only did this king not destroy those who failed him, but from that moment, he planned a rescue for them. Yes, you heard it right, because he could not live knowing all the suffering his children would endure away from him. So, he planned how to free his children from that wicked one.

We should learn from God. When it comes to failures, He knows far more than we do and is our best teacher in dealing with failure. He has never been frustrated by anything we do. He always starts anew with new hope for success and renewed energy. God has never given up, even though there have always been human beings who do not love Him and are ungrateful.

Human beings who think poorly of Him, who blame Him for global disasters like hunger in Africa, earthquakes, and all other worldwide calamities. They blame Him for poverty, diseases, and even mock Him by saying He does not exist.

Despite all this and much more, He does not stand by His heavenly window, indifferent to the world, deciding that the sun should not rise because of His mood. He does not think, "I cannot trust humans; they are all the same—ungrateful and unworthy of my favor. Gabriel, don't let the sun rise today. Send them a storm of thunder to teach them respect. They are all criminals. Let no child be born anymore; in fact, eliminate them all."

God does not think this way, nor does He act on impulses because He does not have such feelings. He is unchangeable, just, and always does things not based on His mood or our actions. He remains in His role as Father even when we stray from our position as His children. Hallelujah!

Don't you feel you need to praise Him? I do. I find joy in serving such a God—one from whom I can learn forgiveness, not to blame others for what happens to me. A God so great that His greatness, power, and, above all, His LOVE cannot be fully described on a paper or with words.

I can only say that at this moment, I feel His Spirit within me and invite you to take a few minutes now to thank Him for being such a good Father. Ask Him to fill you with His warring and conquering spirit, and that all frustration may leave in the name of Jesus. Examine the reasons for your actions. Why do I do the things I do? What are my motives? What do I desire in life? Is your answer to please God? Do you understand the reasons behind your failures and setbacks? Have you learned from them?

A Few Words to Close

I do not pretend to have all the answers for women who suffer, as I have often cried without answers myself. If you are suffering and have a question, I invite you to bring it before God and wait for an answer from Him. Remember, He is alive, interested in you, and wants to help you. If He could change my life and the lives of all the women you've read about in this book, He is willing to do the same with you.

If you have not accepted Him as your Savior, I invite you now to close your eyes and make a prayer of repentance. Seek someone who can help you with your problems and let God, in His mercy, fill you with the joy of His salvation. I declare His power and glory over you. Do not give up or let go; persevere until the end. You are extraordinary. You are a magna woman.

www.ingramcontent.com/pod-product-compliance
Lightning Source LLC
LaVergne TN
LVHW091457170726
843492LV00001B/229

* 9 7 8 9 0 8 3 2 5 2 7 3 5 *